VW BUS
Custom Handbook

VW BUS

Custom Handbook

Laurence Meredith

BAY
VIEW
BOOKS
FROM
MBI Publishing Company

This edition first published in 1994 by Bay View Books Limited, Bideford, Devon, EX39 2PZ England

© Bay View Books Limited, 1994

Published by MBI Publishing Company, 729 Prospect Avenue, PO Box 1, Osceola, WI 54020-0001 USA

Designed by Gerrard Lindley
Typeset by Chris Fayers

MBI Publishing Company books are also available at discounts in bulk quantity for industrial or sales-promotional use. For details write to Special Sales Manager at Motorbooks International Wholesalers & Distributors, 729 Prospect Avenue, PO Box 1, Osceola, WI 54020-0001 USA.

Library of Congress Cataloging-in-Publication Data Available
ISBN 1-870979-47-8

ACKNOWLEDGEMENTS

The author is grateful to the following, without whose help this book would not have been possible: Marc Maskery, Russ Cartwright, Paul Bucket, Holly Keays, Roger Hawes, Chris Trouse, George Shetliffe, Charlie Hamill, Alistair Craig, Peter Stevens, Suzie King, Phil Shaw, Steve Saunders, Steve Newey, Jo Clay, Andy Rice, Mark Pugh, Graham Watson, Simon Holloway, Graham Shears, Geoff Thomas, Alan Schofield, Lee Goodhall, Major Ivan Hirst, Mark Woodward, Tony Woodward, Tim Kemp, German Car Company, Corbeau Seats, Dave Fisher, Tim Jones, Peter Nicholson, and V.A.G. (UK) Ltd.

Printed in China

CONTENTS

INTRODUCTION

The Volkswagen Transporter is one of the few utility vehicles – arguably the only one – to have achieved both classic status and a 'cult' following during its own production lifetime. Throughout the world there are enthusiasts' clubs whose members meet to talk and swap notes about their Buses, so just what is it about the Volkswagen that singles it out for special treatment by the thousands of fans who own and drive a Type 2?

Ask anyone who has spent hundreds of hours in the garage customizing a Crew-cab, caring for a Caravette or putting a Pick-up back together for a reason for doing so and you'll rarely get a straight answer

The affluence and freedom of the 1960s are summed up in this Volkswagen publicity photograph of a Bus ascending an Alpine pass.

because there isn't one. Today there are several manufacturers making compact multi-purpose commercial vehicles, and all are fast, economical, spacious, comfortable and aerodynamically efficient – but Volkswagen made the first, the original and, to many, the very best.

By comparison with the Renault Espace and Toyota Spacecruiser, for example, the Buses made by Volkswagen during the 1950s and '60s are naturally crude, but it would be a smooth-talking salesman

 **VW-TRANSPORTER-SONDERSCHAU**

sehenswert · aufschlußreich · lohnend

Watercolour illustrations featured heavily in Volkswagen's early advertising campaigns

indeed who persuaded a VW nut that he or she ought to go for a 'modern' in place of a vintage Split-screen Camper. And that is because a Volkswagen is always more than a mere form of transport. Like its little sister, the Bug, the Bus has a friendly smiling face, a modest countenance and a trustworthy gait. There's nothing pretentious about a Bus in any shape or form, which is why it has endeared itself to so many people from all walks of life. Like the Bug, it's a vehicle that cuts across social barriers, and whether you're a corporation trash collector or the chairman of a multi-national, there's always a space for you at a Bus meet.

In true Volkswagen tradition, Buses are rugged, reliable, cheap and easy to maintain at home, and extremely durable. Air-cooled engines ensure that there are never any problems with boiling over in summer or freezing up in winter. There are no water hoses to leak or replace, and because the Bus was built like a car, it also drives like one. Despite its tremendous load-carrying capacity, the Type 2 was little longer than a Bug which meant that it was never difficult to park in confined spaces. Everyone's granny could drive the family Bus, even if the sheet metal occasionally acquired a ding here and there, but at least it wasn't like driving a traditional commercial. Light steering, good vision, excellent handling and sure-footed braking all contributed to making the Bus one of the most user-friendly vehicles around.

Restoring a Type 2 isn't just about nostalgia either, because what a really good Bus offers is a highly practical solution to everyday problems in the 1990s. In short, it makes good sense financially and otherwise to own a vehicle which can be used during the work week for carrying goods around and as a family recreation vehicle at the weekend. And if you want to travel afar on a Saturday, you don't have to rush home in the evening because, if you've got yourself a Bus, it doubles as a mobile home, with comfortable beds, washing facilities and every other convenience to enable you to stay put for the night.

Is there really any sense in having a caravan that is used three weeks of the year for a family holiday only to sit in the drive for the rest of the year when, with a Transporter, you have a motorized caravan that can be used every day of the week?

Today, old VW Buses have a brighter future than ever before, and it is clear from recent developments, particularly the growth of recycling that the 'buy-today-throw-away-tomorrow' society is coming to an end. In the 1990s, we are not only restoring our old vehicles but are also preserving them. Discarding something just because it's old isn't sound thinking (as many of our senior citizens will tell you), and thanks to a massive number of far-sighted compa-

nies on both sides of the Atlantic who specialize in the remanufacture of both stock and custom parts, there is now absolutely no need to. It's good news that no matter how old or worn-out your Bus is, it can be fixed. Of course restoring any vehicle properly is likely to be an expensive business, but compare the cost of a ground-up rebuild with the cost of a new vehicle and it will soon become apparent that preserving the past is also financially worthwhile.

Taking the restoration route also has another advantage that few new-car sales executives can offer you, namely, individualistic personalization. If you're in a position to set about rebuilding your own Bus, you can make it to your own spec. There wasn't much wrong with the way Volkswagen made it in the first place, naturally, but if you feel the need for a few more horses under the lid, a little extra rubber on the road and a colour scheme that suits you rather than one that clothed the vehicle originally, you can do it your way and enjoy the feeling that no-one else will be driving a similar vehicle.

A coupé Mercedes may have more style, a Ferrari is a 'little' faster (except in a city traffic jam) and a Cadillac parked in the drive might tell your next door neighbour that you're pretty important, but none of these can match the versatility of a Transporter. Did you ever see anyone take a shower in a Testa Rossa? Come to that, did you ever see anyone fit a picnic hamper into a Testa Rossa?

To use a much-abused and now almost meaningless word, the air-cooled Volkswagen Transporter is a 'classic' in the true sense – and for much the same reason that the Bug is a classic. It was a trend-setter, much copied throughout the globe. It sold in high numbers and opened up doors for millions of people who wouldn't otherwise have even thought of a surfing or camping holiday. Like all true classics, it has bred widespread enthusiasm which, in many instances, borders on obsession. Yes, the Transporter is a big box on wheels but it is a box that was beautifully executed, and for many it has never been equalled.

Throughout this book I have attempted to convey some of the many reasons why Transporters continue to form the centrepiece of so many lives, and in doing so have unashamedly allowed my own enthusiasm for virtually anything with a VW roundel on its nose to creep into the text. Naturally I can't apologize for that, but I mention it as a friendly warning to readers who may have the misguided impression that journalists are unbiased reporters of hard information.

Laurence Meredith
January 1994

THE TRANSPORTER STORY

For most German people who had survived the devastation of a six-year war, life was still pretty grim after the cessation of hostilities in 1945. The minds of ordinary Germans were sharply focussed on the urgent need to find food to eat, but the only way this great country was going to recover properly was by the complete restoration of its industry, communications networks and transport.

Few private German citizens in 1945 could afford to buy motor cars. Thanks to the efforts of the British army, production of the Beetle was resumed after the War but the initial batches were destined for the occupation forces, which meant that the indigenous population had either to walk or repair what motorized transport they had with whatever tools and equipment they could find.

When the Volkswagen factory at Wolfsburg was put under the control of Major Ivan Hirst of the Royal Electrical and Mechanical Engineers it was inevitable that once full-scale production of the Beetle was under way, some form of transport would be needed within the factory to take components to and from the various assembly lines. At first there were a few electric-powered vehicles but they were in short supply, so Major Hirst borrowed a number of British-made forklift trucks from the army — which was a great help except that it wasn't long before the army asked for them back. This left the factory being run with virtually no means of internal transport, and an alternative to borrowed trucks had to be found. The people who worked in the experimental shop hastily sketched out an idea for a vehicle which utlized a Kübelwagen chassis and a driver's seat at the rear, and when put into practice it worked exceptionally well.

Some time later, the Dutch Volkswagen importer, Ben Pon (who incidentally started selling Volkswagens in Holland from 1947) saw some of these peculiar vehicles, which in concept were similar to the tricycles used by window cleaners, milkmen and other tradesmen in his own country. After putting two and two together he came up with the idea for an all-purpose load carrier which he roughly sketched out on a piece of paper. The sketch still exists to this day and bears a remarkable similarity to the vehicle which would one day become the world's best-selling light commercial.

Ben Pon discussed his idea with Colonel Charles

By 1947 the Wolfsburg factory, which was badly damaged during Allied bombing raids in 1944, had been virtually rebuilt and Beetle production continued at the rate of around 250 cars per day, but it would be three years before the start of Transporter production.

Radclyffe, who had overall responsibility for light engineering in the British occupation zone, but the factory was already over-stretched making Beetles and Radclyffe reluctantly had to say no. But Pon's scheme appealed strongly to Heinz Nordhoff, who took over as Chief Executive of Volkswagen on January 1 1948, and within a short time Nordhoff and Volkswagen's chief development engineer, Alfred Heasner, set the ball rolling for Pon's idea to be put into practice.

On November 20 1948, the first blueprints for the Transporter arrived on Nordhoff's desk. They showed almost identical models, the only difference between the two, other than the cab design, being

After the War, flatbed trucks were used around the factory and inspired the Dutch Volkswagen importer, Ben Pon, to come up with the idea for a Beetle-based Transporter.

Ben Pon sketched out his idea for a multi-purpose Panelvan in a notebook. His drawing bears a remarkable resemblance to the vehicle that would eventually go into production.

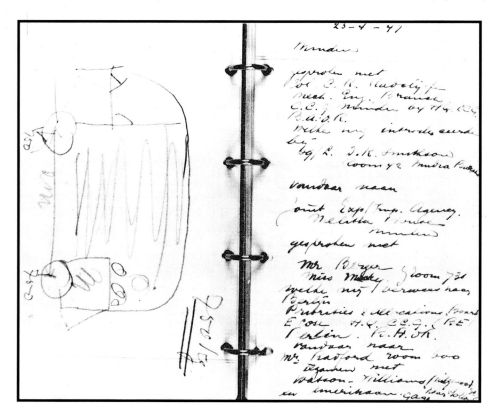

This 1949 prototype is without a rear window, has a large petrol filler neck high up on the rear quarter and is without a rear bumper, but the concept of a 'box on wheels' was correct first time.

that one drawing was marked 'A' and the other was marked 'B'. Model 'B' was chosen because the cab had a slight curve at the front without an overhanging roof.

At a meeting of February 7 1949, Nordhoff suggested separating the seat in the cab in order to make a driver's seat and a two-seater bench for passengers. This had the advantage that the bench seat could be easily removed from the cab. After just two days, the technical department threw out his plan as unworkable but the idea was eventually introduced on the 1962 model.

Initial tests of the new vehicle came to a halt on April 5 1949. The unmodified Bug floorpan could not withstand the load stresses of the new bodywork. A new prototype was hastily built but with unitary construction. The body and chassis were welded together and were strengthened with an additional subframe incorporating two steel rails running north-to-south and five crossmembers between the front and rear axles.

An added challenge was the ratio of total weight to empty weight. The first test prototype had a ratio of 1.85:1 which was raised to 1.91:1 with the unitary construction model. The brakes were improved and fuel consumption was reduced due to the improved body shape. At the same time, the front axle and shock absorbers were strengthened and reduction gears, similar to those used on the wartime Kübelwagens, were fitted to the rear wheels to give better acceleration from the 1131cc engine, but even so top speed of the first production models was only around 50mph/80kmh.

Other improvements included the following: 1) The pedals were better spaced due to the enhanced curvature of the car. 2) The heater for the windshield

The reduction gearboxes fitted to the outer ends of the drive-shafts helped with acceleration, but were discontinued when the Bay-window model was introduced in 1967. The gearbox shown here with a one-piece casing is from a post-1959 model.

Largely made of alloy, but with cast iron cylinder barrels, the Transporter's engine was 'borrowed' from the Beetle and initially produced 25bhp. Up until May 1959, the generator pedestal was cast into the crankcase.

and driver were combined. 3) The profile of the seats was improved. 4) The cab doors were made lighter and more rigid. 5) Awkward corners in the loading bay were 'ironed out' and the luggage space above the engine was enlarged. 6) In view of a potential threat from foreign competition, two swing-doors were fitted to the loading bay.

The unitary construction prototype covered 12,000 kilometres of testing on Volkswagen's track and, on May 19 1949, Heinz Nordhoff announced that production would start on November 1 or December 1949 at the latest.

Following Nordhoff's announcement in May 1949, the experimental department received orders to build four demonstration vans along with two more test vehicles. These were 'closed' Panelvans but two were to be built with special interiors and one was to be a 'minibus' with seating for up to eight or nine people.

Nordhoff then suggested that the top of the engine bay should be lowered in height and an additional panel be built to isolate the interior of the vehicle from the heat produced by the engine. A further prototype therefore came into being on August 31 1949.

After aerodynamic experiments, the shape of the new prototype had reduced the drag factor down from 0.75 on the first vehicle to 0.44 on the unitary construction prototype. A limiter was therefore fitted as the speed for a loaded van had risen to 53mph/86kmh and to 57mph/92kmh for an unladen van.

During a press conference on November 12 1949, Nordhoff presented the first Volkswagen Transporter and said in a speech on that occasion, "Like our Bug is a car without compromises, so will our Transporter be without compromises. This is why we did not start from an available chassis but from the cargo space. This is the clean, no-compromise principle of our Transporter. With this van and only this van, the cargo space lies exactly between the axles. In the front sits the driver and, in the back is the same weight due to the engine and fuel tank. That is the best compromise... We would have put the engine in the front without hesitation if this had been a better solution. However, the famous 'cab above the engine' gave such horrendous handling characteristics when loaded that we never even considered it. You can tell by the trees in the British zone how well the army lorries, built with this principle, handle on wet roads when they are not loaded."

Built with the object of carrying a load equal to its own weight, the Transporter's 162cu.ft of loadspace was almost two-thirds of the vehicle's total volume. In other words, it was a box on wheels. With its engine in the rear and passengers placed up front over the axle, the Transporter, with the payload carried between the axles, was perfectly balanced. It was also exceptionally easy to load thanks to its side doors. If you used it for camping, for delivering goods or anything else, the Transporter was a masterpiece of automotive design work.

Mechanically, it differed very little from the Beetle right up to the 1970s as both shared the same parts bin. The original air-cooled flat-four 1131cc

OHV engine produces 25bhp at 3300rpm and is bolted to a four-speed 'crash' gearbox at the rear. A compact but highly unconventional design, the engine comprises a two-piece light alloy crankcase split vertically on the centre line through the main bearings and bolted together.

The short crankshaft runs in three main bearings made of thin wall steel backed with copper lead inserts, with a fourth bearing that acts as a support for the auxiliary drives. Mounted directly below the crankshaft, the camshaft runs in the crankcase without separate bearings and is driven by the crankshaft with single helical gears. Each cam operates two pushrods, which are encased in cylindrical tubes beneath the cast-iron cylinder barrels. The pushrods, in turn, operate the valves via conventional rockers.

Until May 1959, when the 34bhp 1200cc engine was introduced with wedge-shaped combustion chambers, both the 25bhp and subsequent 30bhp engines had hemispherical combustion chambers and light alloy, flat-topped pistons. Light alloy was used for the cylinder heads which, like the crankcase and cylinder barrels, are liberally finned to aid engine cooling. Interestingly, both the inlet and exhaust valves have a 28.6mm diameter.

Driven by spiral gears from the crankshaft, the distributor is bolted to the top of the left-hand side of the crankcase and in turn, drives the mechanical fuel pump, also bolted to the top of the crankcase, via an operating rod. Fuel from the single downdraught Solex carburettor is dispensed to the combustion chambers through an inlet manifold which branches into two pipes immediately below the carburettor. The pipes are bolted to the top of each cylinder head and deliver the fuel/air mixture through a single port which was modified to a dual-port arrangement for the 1600 engine in 1970.

Engine cooling is dependent upon air drawn in through louvers in the bodywork by a fan which is mounted vertically in a purpose-built sheet steel housing on top of the engine. Attached to the dynamo armature shaft and driven by a fan belt attached to the crankshaft and dynamo pulley wheels, the fan blows cold air over the oil cooler, which is bolted to the left-hand side of the crankcase, and over the cylinder barrels and heads. Hot air is expelled at the rear of the bodywork and is prevented from entering the engine compartment and causing overheating by steel 'trays', which are bolted over the top of the cylinder barrels and at the rear of the engine.

Heating for the cabin is provided by air passing over the cylinder barrels and heads. A control knob in the cabin is attached to a steel cable, which closes off a cooling air outlet flap and, at the same time, opens a heat control valve. Hot air is then ducted into the cabin via heater boxes which are integrated into the exhaust pipes of the front pair of cylinders. The system was modified in 1963. Instead of heater boxes, there were heat exchangers, which took the form of large chambers built around the exhaust pipes. The new arrangement had the advantage of providing 'fresh' air in the cabin, rather than air that had been passed over the engine as previously. One of the criticisms aimed at early Transporters and Beetles, was that if and when the engine became encrusted in mud and oil, the odours emanating from both were picked up by the heating system and caused discomfort to drivers and passengers. With heat exchangers, the problem disappeared overnight.

Lubricating oil, which is partially responsible for cooling the engine, is circulated by a gear-type oil pump at the rear of the crankcase driven by the camshaft. The oil is pumped from the bottom of the crankcase through holes in the latter to the crankshaft, camshaft and pushrods. There is no conventional oil filter: a small removeable gauze in the bottom of the engine suffices. In total, the engine is lubricated by just four and a half pints of oil and Volkswagen recommended from the outset that a monograde was preferable to a multigrade.

The four-speed gearbox is mated and secured to the engine with four bolts and is protected from mechanical vibrations by rubber mountings. Made of light alloy, the gearbox casing is in two pieces and split vertically and longitudinally. The starter motor is housed on the top right-hand side.

Built into the gearbox is the differential assembly which consists of the differential housing, side gears, pinions and pinion shaft, universal joint assemblies and swing axles. Engine torque is taken up through a single plate, cable-operated Fichtel & Sachs dry clutch, which is splined to the gearbox input shaft. Over-engineered to the point of being almost 'bullet-proof', a stock Transporter gearbox in good condition can accept power outputs of up to 150bhp.

From May 1959 (chassis number 469 506), the Transporter's gearbox was modified, with a one-piece casing instead of two as previously. Synchromesh was introduced on all four forward speeds, and because much larger differential side bearings were used, it was possible to remove the driveshafts without having to dismantle the entire assembly as was the case with the original gearbox.

Following Beetle practice, torsion bar springing was employed at the front and the rear. Encased in two cylindrical and transversely positioned tubes one above the other at the front, the torsion springs are bolted on their outer ends to trailing arms, which in turn are secured by bolts to the hubs. The shock absorbers are mounted on steel 'uprights' that form part of the front axle assembly. At the rear, the torsion springs are also encased in single cylindrical

A fire tender was one of the several special Transporters built by Volkswagen for German public services.

The Kombi was an obvious choice for Germany's ambulance service. This American owned vehicle is a post-1962 model with large round indicators above the headlamps.

Rear suspension (left) is by torsion bars, trailing arms and swinging half-axles. The driveshafts, which run in cylindrical tubes, are connected to reduction gearboxes in the hubs.

Classic Porsche-designed front suspension (above) utilizes torsion leaves housed in the upper and lower tubes linked to trailing arms on their outer ends. This is a 1967 beam which is also fitted with a stabilizer bar.

tubes and are positioned transversely in front of the gearbox.

Steering is courtesy of a transverse link and unequal length track rods. Connection to the front hubs is by king and link pins which were changed for balljoints on the Bay-window models in 1967. The steering gearbox itself, which is mounted firmly to the chassis frame head, is a worm and nut affair but was changed in 1961 for a 'drag-free' worm and roller unit.

Hydraulically operated single-circuit drum brakes were initially employed on all four wheels and the design of the system is entirely conventional. Dual-circuit brakes were introduced for the 1968 model year and discs were fitted at the front in place of drums in 1970.

Naturally, Volkswagen continued to make improvements to the basic design throughout the Transporter's life but by and large the concept remained unchanged for many, many years.

As you might expect, there were several further changes made between the prototype stage and the first production vehicles, including repositioning the fuel filler neck from high up on the outside of the left-hand rear panel to inside the engine compartment on the left-hand side, a move that necessitated moving the spare wheel, initially situated vertically on the right of the engine compartment, to a horizontal position above the engine.

The large 'Barn door' to the engine compartment was redesigned, as were many other features as we

Completely restored front suspension with new king and link pins, central swivel pin and brake components. Balljoints replaced king and link pins with the introduction of the Bay-window Bus.

An early production Panelvan with opening side doors for 'kerbside' access to the 162cu ft loadspace. Being purely a functional vehicle, the bodywork is devoid of chrome embellishments.

shall see in due course. In fact, the design was so successful that the 100,000th unit had been produced at Wolfsburg by October 9 1954. In 1956 production was completely transferred to a purpose-built factory in Hanover – but we are jumping the gun a little.

Volkswagen officially unveiled the Transporter, Type 2 or Bus, call it what you will, on November 12 1949, the first production models being offered for sale to the public from March the following year. Initially only a Panelvan was available, but it was soon followed in May 1950, by a Kombi, which came with side windows and removable seats in the load area, and in June by the Microbus, which came as a 7-, 8- or 9-seater with an improved level of trim. Nicknamed 'Bulli' in Germany and 'Breadloaf' in Denmark, Volkswagen's Transporter was an instant success as a load carrier for people and goods alike, and by the end of 1950, just six years after the end of the War, some 60 Type 2s were rolling off the Wolfsburg assembly lines every day of the week.

Nordhoff himself once remarked, "When a box on wheels is the basic need, a box on wheels is the perfect answer", but one of the principal reasons for Volkswagen's Bus becoming a collector's item is that it was the leader which other manufacturers could only emulate. To enthusiasts today, the Bulli or Bulldog is much more than an everyday workhorse for carting cargo around or taking the family on a camping weekend. For those who remember the good old Splitties as a common sight on European,

Known as the 'Barndoor', the top-hinged engine lid on pre-1955 Transporters is enormous and has a single brake light mounted above the number plate. There is no opening hatch at this stage.

American and British soil, today's 'Bullimania' is about reliving the past and recapturing the spirit of some of the best days of the 20th century.

The most desirable of the early Transporters, the Microbus or Samba, was introduced in April 1951 with production continuing right through to 1967 when the Bay-window models replaced the Split-screens. A superb vehicle, it was designed to carry up to nine people and boasted a full-length canvas sunroof. A number of additional windows gave improved all-round vision, and there were four rectangular, curved windows built into each side of the roof. The Samba also acquired a full-width dashboard while other, more basic models in the range made do with a speedometer behind the steering wheel.

One of the most successful models in the Transporter range was launched in September 1952 in the shape of the Pick-up truck. Versatile, and blessed with the ability to go almost anywhere, the Pick-up endeared itself to all sorts of tradesmen because it could not only accommodate three hefty guys and their tools but would also stand up to truly horrendous quantities of abuse for considerably longer than anything else available. Who doesn't remember the sight of a gang of builders going off to work early in the morning with a ton or more of sand piled high on the back of the truck, a concrete-mixer balanced on top and plumes of cigarette smoke billowing from

Pre-1955 Panelvans are easily distinguished by the lack of fresh air eyebrows above the windshield. Note the early style bumpers and the mirror arms fitted to the windshield pillars.

The Kombi, launched in May 1950, came with side windows and removable seats and was followed by the Microbus in June 1950, with an improved level of trim.

Top-of-the-range Microbus (below) has a full-width dashboard while all other models up to 1955 make do with a separate speedometer placed behind the steering wheel.

Most sought after Bus of all, the Samba (above) sports additional roof windows, a rolltop sunroof and a high level of trim.

With seating for up to nine, the Microbus (below) was among the first multi-purpose vehicles.

the cab windows? Often the rear wheels were so drunkenly decambered under the excessive weight that anyone who didn't know how Volkswagen really build cars could be forgiven for thinking that the whole ensemble might grind to a halt under the strain. Yet somehow it never happened, and each evening the same gang of builders would return home without their sand at three times the speed at which they had left for work 10 hours earlier. After many years of similar abuse and hard work, the old truck would be sold on to be subjected to the same brutal treatment in someone else's hands but rarely broke down and was always ready for more work next morning.

The Pick-up was an obvious model choice from the beginning but it presented a few major design problems which first had to be overcome. In order to offer a reasonably sized load platform at a sensible height, both the fuel tank and the spare wheel had to be relocated. The fuel tank was moved forward to a position over the gearbox, rather than over the top of the engine, and the spare wheel was placed behind the locker bed.

The Pick-up's new fuel tank arrangement was adopted across the range in 1955 because it meant that the large and heavy rear Barn door could be replaced by an opening rear window and a much smaller engine lid. Opening rear windows, incidentally, were something of a rarity on early Transporters but were eventually offered as an optional extra.

Also in 1952, the four-speed gearbox was treated to synchromesh on all forward speeds except bottom, a great advantage to the surprisingly large number of folks whose motoring careers had been characterised by their unending ability to crunch and scrape a conventional 'box to an audibly premature death.

By this time, Volkswagen had launched an ambulance version of the Transporter as well, appropriately fitted out but with its rear door opening downwards rather than upwards.

Having soldiered on with the 1131cc 25bhp engine for too long, the factory took the decision in 1954 to increase the power output of both the Bug and the Bus by increasing the motor's cubic capacity to 1192cc. At the same time the compression ratio was raised from 5.8:1 to 6.6:1, and the result was a useful gain in maximum power from 25 to 30bhp, which was achieved at 3400rpm. As the engines and gearboxes fitted to the Bus at this stage were identical to those of the Bug, it was inevitable that their mechanical development would run roughly parallel, but whereas the Bug was fitted with dual tailpipes the Split-screen Bus always had just one. Right-hand-drive versions also became available on all models in 1954 to cater for the British market.

As with the Bug, modifications were made to the

Bus range continuously and most were very small detail improvements. New models and major changes were by and large announced in August of each year after the factory's annual holidays, but there were exceptions, as in 1955, when March was the chosen month. In fact 1955 is thought of as something of a watershed year in the development of the Bus because the vehicles made after March were so very different that virtually no components were

Launched in 1952, the Pick-up truck presented design problems which necessitated resiting spare wheel and fuel tank. The locker bed is for storing tools and equipment.

The wide-bodied Pick-up was particularly popular with the building trade.

The 100,000th Transporter rolls off the Wolfsburg assembly lines on October 9 1954, two years before production was transferred to a purpose-built factory at Hanover.

Perfection: a vintage Samba with American-spec bumpers, lots of chrome and 'Safari' opening windows.

Early Hella tail lamps were neat, small and not immediately visible to following traffic.

interchangeable with the pre-'55 range.

Following on from the lead taken by the Pick-up three years earlier, the fuel tank was repositioned above the gearbox and the spare wheel was moved behind the driver's seat. Moving the tank meant that the engine deck could be lowered which, in turn, allowed for the fitment of a useful tailgate above the separate engine lid. A full-width dashboard was fitted across the range, whereas previously it was only available with the deluxe Microbus, and a new ventilation system was also introduced which saw a revision in the frontal appearance of the cab. Post-March 1955 vehicles have twin grilles above the windscreen giving the characteristic and pretty 'peaked' front.

The chassis was made much stronger, and although cross-ply tires were retained (what else in 1955?) the 5-bolt pressed steel wheels were reduced in diameter from 16 to 15 inches. By this stage the Bus had become a much more modern vehicle. It was more rugged, faster, the fuel consumption had improved a little thanks to the more powerful engine, and it was generally better equipped than before. The bodywork modifications made the Bus look less austere and less functional. In practice it was as functional as ever but a lot of attention had been paid by the stylists to making the Bus more aesthetically pleasing, and although the pre-'55 Buses are now very rare and much treasured by collectors, the Transporters made between 1955 and 1967 are not only more plentiful but also by far the most practical of the vintage variety.

Having gone through the traumas of setting up a brand new production plant at Hanover in 1956, Volkswagen's engineers justifiably had something of a rest for a couple of years and there were relatively few modifications to the Transporter. In any case, modifications weren't really necessary at the time either. Considering the traffic conditions, the Suez crisis of 1956 and the purpose for which most Transporters were then used, the specification was pretty much dead right.

The bumpers were changed in 1958 from the old grooved pattern to a plainer, bigger and heavier type and, in the same year, vehicles destined for North America were fitted with what are universally known simply as 'American-spec' bumpers, which were distinguished by an additional bar running above the main blade and through extended and much taller overriders. At the rear, there were changes to the lights. Whereas before 1958 there was a separate brake light positioned in the middle of the panelwork, the stop light was now sensibly incorporated into the main light assemblies, but the semaphore indicators were retained in the 'B' posts for another couple of years.

The now-trendy Crew-cab or Double-cab Pick-up was added to the range in 1958 and was designed to

The Double-cab or Crew-cab was added to the range in 1958, and with seating for up to six it appealed to tradesmen working in small gangs. This restored example is fitted with an optional tarpaulin.

appeal to the sort of tradesmen who worked in small gangs. It retained the versatility of the regular Pick-up truck but with its revised cab could carry twice as many passengers.

In the fast-moving world of motor manufacturing, the factory couldn't allow the grass to grow under its feet and in May '59 the Bus range was fitted with an all-new engine and transmission (from chassis 469-506). The basic layout remained the same as ever but there were so many detail improvements that very few components were interchangeable between the two types.

The engine, which now developed 34bhp, had a more rugged crankcase with heavier studs and bolts, a stronger crankshaft, a different fuel pump, a detachable generator pedestal (replacing the type cast as one piece with the crankcase) and wider spacing between the cylinders to give improved cooling. The cylinder heads were also redesigned, with wedge-shaped combustion chambers, and the valves were repositioned at an angle.

Although the new engine retained the same 1192cc capacity, power output was improved thanks to an increase in the compression ratio. A smaller crankshaft pulley and a larger generator pulley were fitted which reduced the speed of the cooling fan and thus made the engine a little quieter than previously. The 34bhp engine was an extremely good power unit and although the additional 4bhp was not exactly breathtaking in its effect on acceleration and top speed, it was nonetheless worthwhile.

As mentioned above, the transmission was changed at the same time. Out went the old splitcase design and in came the new tunnel type with detachable side plates and synchromesh on all four forward speeds. Outwardly resembling that of the

Porsche 356, the new transmission was stronger and a good deal easier to service. The driveshafts could now be removed without having to take the whole assembly apart, saving time for mechanics and money for customers. However, the reduction gears in the hubs were retained right until the end of Split-tie production in 1967.

During the first 10 years of production, Volkswagen built and sold 678,000 Transporters in all their many guises and, in August 1961, celebrated the production of its one millionth unit, a long way behind the remarkable Bug, production of which had reached 827,000 in 1961 alone, but an achievement just the same.

By 1960, the semaphore arms had given way to more modern flashing indicators. At the front, there were what are commonly referred to as the bullet-type of flasher, a neat torpedo-shaped pod mounted high on the front panel. At the rear, the turn indicators were incorporated into the stop and tail light assemblies.

An amber segment in the rear lights wasn't added until 1962, in which year the front flashers were changed again, this time for large round disc flashers that remained in place until 1967. Also in 1962, a high-roof version of the Panelvan was introduced which gave six cubic metres of load volume. The raised roof was useful for all sorts of different reasons but the vehicle particularly appealed to people in the clothing trade because it allowed for garment rails to be fitted. Today the 'High-tops', as they are affectionately known, are particularly rare, the vast majority having led hard lives.

By the early to mid 1960s the question of safety in road transport had become a hotly-debated public issue. Consumer groups then, as now, were able to put considerable pressure, if indirectly, upon motor manufacturers to mend their ways. Slowly but surely, cars and commercials began to change purely to meet the needs of safety-inspired legislation, and to that end Volkswagen made several improvements in 1963.

The old flip-out cab door handles were replaced by the push-button type and both the tailgate and rear window were widened. At the same time, the tailgate became self-supporting on torsion struts in place of the sliding stay, and the intake louvres for directing cool air into the engine were cut to face inwards rather than outwards as previously, though quite why the latter was considered a safety improvement is not at all easy to appreciate.

Sliding side loading doors were available as an option in May 1963 before the general revisions in

Bullet-type indicators (top) replaced semaphore arms in 1960 and were fitted above the headlamps. An amber segment for the rear flashing indicators wasn't added until 1962.

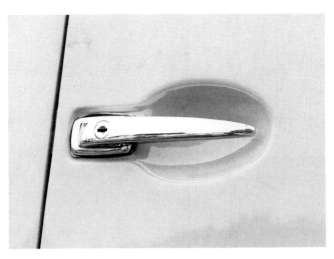

Just three years after the bullet-type indicators were introduced, large disc-shaped flashers replaced them.

In 1963 the old pull-out cab door handles (above) were replaced by the pushbutton type (below).

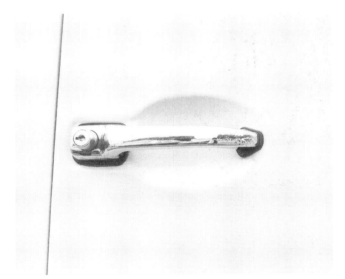

A late addition to the range, a High-roof van was launched in 1962 and proved particularly popular with the rag trade as garment rails could be fitted in the load area. Now rare, many High-roofs led hard lives.

The small rear window (left) of the early model was enlarged considerably in August 1963 (above).

The early, outward-facing engine air-intake louvres (top) were replaced in 1963 by a less stylish, inward facing arrangement (above).

August. Incidentally, the side doors were always placed on the right-hand side of left-hand-drive Buses and on the left-hand side of right-hand-drive vehicles from the beginning, but some Transporters were fitted with doors on both sides as an optional extra.

Also in 1963 the road wheels were reduced in diameter again, this time from 15 inches to 14. They still retained the 5-bolt fixing unlike the Bug, which got 4-bolt wheels on the 1500 from 1966. As with the Bug, the V-over-W motif in the centre of the hubcaps was no longer highlighted after 1963, presumably in an effort to save paint. And a brief word about hub-caps: lesser models in the range usually had them painted whereas those fitted to the Microbuses were chromium-plated.

By far the most important happening of 1963 though was the introduction of the 1500 versions. Until this time, Volkswagen customers had had a wide choice in body styles and a reasonably good selection of trim levels, but when it came to engines, you got a 1200 and that was that. The new 1500, which was sold alongside the 1200 for a couple of years, was a great improvement. Although at first it only produced 42bhp, it was a good deal more pow-erful than the 34bhp unit.

Whereas the 1200 was known as the three-quarter ton Transporter, the new 1500 became the one-ton Transporter, and because of its extra power it came in for a number of modifications under the skin. The brakes were uprated, the suspension was made stiffer with progressive bump stops and the gearing was altered. Strangely enough, although the overall gearing of the 1500 was taller, the final drive ratio was lower, with higher ratios adopted for the reduc-tion gears.

The 1500 engine had been 'borrowed' from the Type 3 saloon which Volkswagen introduced in 1961, and the result was improved torque across the rev range and a higher top speed. Maximum speed on the 1500 is governed to 65mph, which is also its cruising speed, but it is possible to reach higher speeds by the simple expedient of removing the gov-ernor. It goes without saying that if this is done you need to take great care not to over-rev the engine, particularly when accelerating up through the gears.

Seemingly pleased with their efforts in 1963, Volkswagen's engineers appear to have taken some-thing of a rest for 1964, and 1965 for that matter, save that the 1200 was dropped from the range com-pletely, leaving the 1500 to beat a sales path on its own. Curiously the 1300 engine which found its way into the rear end of the Bug in 1965 was never installed in the Transporter even though it devel-oped only 2bhp less than the 1500 unit.

On to 1966, when the tailgate lock was changed for the second time in almost as many years. Before 1963, the tailgate was opened by turning a T-handle, which was changed to a push-button in August of that year, but by 1966 a small finger latch had been installed which was considered safer and more likely to deter would-be car thieves. A column-mounted stalk at last replaced the old foot-operated dipswitch and in August 1967 12-volt electrics arrived to replace the 6-volt system that had struggled (sometimes unsuccessfully) to provide the sparks for so long. Anyone who has experienced the dubious pleasure of driving at night for any length of time behind 6-volt headlights fitted with standard bulbs will recall what a pleasure it was to get behind the wheel of a 12-volter, although even the 12-volt headlamps leave a great deal to be desired by the standards of the 1990s.

So, some 17 years after the first Transporters rolled off the Wolfsburg assembly lines, the era of the Split-screen classic was nearing its end. After the production of 1.8 million, the last Splittie was built in July 1967 to make way for a replacement and very different model. The dividing line between the two halves of the windshield, which above all else had given the 'box on wheels' such great character, would never be seen on a new production Volkswagen again. The era of the Bay-windows was about to begin.

In 1963 a push-button replaced the old turning T-handle on the tailgate.

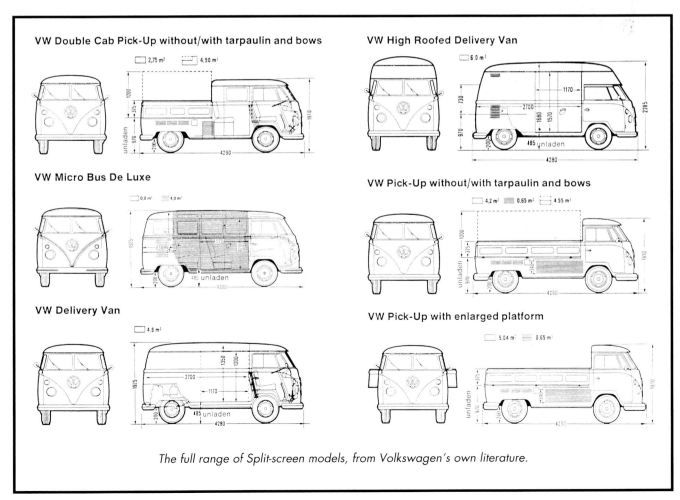

The full range of Split-screen models, from Volkswagen's own literature.

Second Generation, 1967-79

Having started with a clean sheet of drawing paper, Volkswagen launched the second-generation Transporter in August 1967, and despite less appealing body styling it was generally well received by the press and the public. Often referred to these days as the Bay-window model for rather obvious reasons, the 'Mk 2' version was a huge improvement in virtually every way over the Split-screen models.

Lengthened by 100mm/4in overall, the new bodyshell boasted a curved one-piece windshield, a larger rear window, improved interior ventilation with twin intake grilles moved below the windshield, and a sliding side door as a standard fitment. The front indicators were placed below the headlights and the wrap-round front bumper incorporated a step on each side to make it easier to climb into the cab.

Both the Kombi and the Clipper (the Bay-window equivalent of the Samba) had larger side windows, while the dashboard was redesigned and was even padded over the top and the ignition/starter switch was built into the steering column.

Pneumatically operated twin-jet windscreen washers were new additions, the dashboard control switches were marked with symbols and the ashtray, according to the VW brochure, was 'Designed for

smokers – by a smoker'. Separate seats up in the cab meant that access to the load area could be gained more easily. With the emphasis very much more on safety than in the early days of the decade, there were dozens and dozens of detail improvements.

At the rear, the old swing axles, which had been a bone of contention amongst critics from the early days of the Bug, were modified and became double-jointed. In principle, they were still swing axles, but, being double-jointed, they were less likely to be affected by sudden changes of wheel camber. In other words, if you had your foot hard on the gas pedal in a corner and the tail began to work a little too hard for its living, you were less likely to be treated to the dreaded wheel 'tuck-in'. Apart from being double-jointed, the new layout differed from the conventional one in having an additional semi-trailing arm which located the rear wheel instead of an axle tube as previously.

Other chassis modifications included an increase in the front and rear track, the deletion of the reduction gears altogether, the replacement of kingpins with maintenance free ball joints and the fitment of

Launched in August 1967, the Bay-window model was bigger and much improved. The fresh air grilles were moved to the front panel, the indicators were positioned below the headlamps, the bumpers were stronger and the one-piece windshield offered better forward vision, but the domed hubcaps remained for another three years.

As comprehensive as ever, the range basically comprises Panelvan (including High-roof), Microbus, Kombi, Double-cab and Single-cab Pick-up.

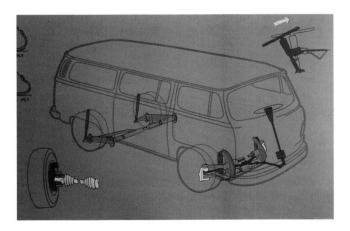

The chassis was improved with double-jointed driveshafts which helped to prevent the dreaded wheel 'tuck in', and at the front there were maintenance-free balljoints to replace king and link pins.

A period Motor Show shot at the British launch of the Bay-window model, which is now fitted with a sliding door.

a dual-circuit braking system. If one circuit failed, you still had another one to back it up. Again, most of these improvements were also incorporated into the Bug at the same time, and many of the parts, including the new headlights, are interchangeable between the two vehicles. A large parts bin is a necessity when you produce as many different vehicles as Volkswagen.

The new model was also given more power courtesy of the 1600cc engine, which was similar to the one fitted by this time to the Type 3 car. With a compression ratio of 7.7:1, the 1584cc power unit developed 47bhp at 4000rpm and gave the Bus a top speed, according to Volkswagen, of 65mph/105kmh. In reality, most Transporters of this generation will easily top 70mph/113kmh and more, but Volkswagen were never in the habit of exaggerating performance figures.

As you might expect, the range was just as comprehensive as previously and included a Panelvan (also available with a high roof), a Pick-up, a Double-cab, an extended-platform Pickup, and either an eight- or nine-seat Bus with a choice of two trim levels.

If the specification on paper looked like an impressive improvement, driving a Bay was even more so even if the new model lacked a lot of the character of the old Splittie. Jump into the cab and you instantly had a feeling of space. All-round visibility was superb and the 'panoramic' windshield was a vast improvement when it came to checking the traffic flow from the right and left at a busy junction.

The extra power from the engine made overtaking a lot safer and, thanks to the revised rear axle layout, roadholding and handling became a good deal more neutral. As ever, top speed and maximum cruising speed were the same and despite the extra weight of the new vehicle it was still capable of returning 27mpg.

Optional extras included a steel sliding sunroof (standard on the Clipper model), a front passenger bench seat (standard in the Pick-up), a booster fan for ventilating air, radio, auxiliary heater, electrically-heated rear window, hazard warning lights and additional instrument panel padding to name but a few.

With a payload of one ton and a load space of 177cu. ft (or 219cu. ft. with the High-roof van), the new range of Transporters still led the rest of the

There is more space and comfort in the cab of the Bay-window model and the moulded dashboard is more comprehensively laid out, but in modernizing the Bus, the feeling of 'cosiness' to which Splittie owners had become accustomed was lost.

world in the light commercial-cum-leisure market in just about every market in which it was sold.

In January 1968, the roof on the High-top was made from fibreglass to save weight, and other detail improvements continued to be made across the range. Particular attention was paid to sound insulation of the cab and the wheel arches were also damped with rubber.

Under the slogan 'More safety, more comfort', further changes were made in August 1969. The doors were strengthened to give better protection to passengers against side impacts, the bodyshell was made more rigid and therefore stronger, and a collapsible steering column was fitted across the entire range. These were very much under-the-skin improvements because visually nothing much happened at all. And it was the same the following year save that the improvements could really be felt.

In August 1970, engine performance was improved yet again when the 1584cc engine gained dual-port cylinder heads and pushed out a full 50bhp at 4000rpm. The revised heads allowed the engine to breathe more freely and made a big difference to the feel of the vehicle on the road but, as usual, there was a downside: the dual-porters have a tendency to suffer from cracked cylinder heads, especially on high-mileage examples, but replacements are cheap enough.

Further changes in August 1970 included a change from drum to disc brakes at the front, a brake power regulator for the rear axle, stronger driveshafts, wider tyres, and flat hubcaps in place of the stylish domed variety that saw service on the Bug up to 1965. It's interesting that whereas the Bug gained front disc brakes in 1966 on the 1500 model, the Transporter had to wait another four years before being similarly equipped. During 1970 Volkswagen celebrated the manufacture of its three millionth Transporter, but it would be another five years before the fourth million rolled off the line.

In 1971 a 1.7-litre (1679cc) engine was offered as an option, differing from conventional Bug and Bus practice in having the cooling fan mounted on the nose of the crankshaft, in the interests of saving space, rather than in the upright position. The larger engine first saw service in the Type 4 passenger saloon launched in 1968. As fitted to the Bus it developed 66bhp and offered a maximum speed in the region of 78mph/125kmh. Is that supposed to be impressive? You bet, especially considering the

Business and tradesmen welcomed the new Panelvan with open arms because of the increased loadspace – up to 177cu.ft. In 1969, the body was made more rigid, the doors were strengthened and a collapsible safety steering column was fitted.

By the end of the 1960s, Volkswagen's Bus was used throughout the world for an increasingly wide variety of purposes including hotel taxi work, more traditionally the domain of Mercedes-Benz saloons.

For the 1973 model year there were many detail improvements including thicker brake pads, the indicators were repositioned above the headlamps instead of below, and the cab step was cleverly sited inside the door.

By 1970, there were dozens of companies specializing in Camper conversions to meet demand. The large side-elevating roof shown here was particularly popular as it was easy to operate and offered lots of headroom. Note that flat hubcaps have replaced the domed variety.

engine was propelling a body that was about as aerodynamically efficient as a house brick. Also in '71, all models were fitted with larger rear lights, soundproofing was further improved and the fuel filler neck was relocated further back in the body, well out of the way of the sliding door. Strange it took so long.

The quest to produce an even safer vehicle was continued through the following year when, in August 1972, the Transporter gained a deformable crumple zone in the cab floor, a feature which we all take for granted in our daily cars today. But this was over 20 years ago, and the idea of deformable steel structures was then new and revolutionary in the motor industry. Yet although the 1972 Bus range was in many ways the best that Volkswagen had ever made, we know today that it was also the rustiest. A number of experts have offered their reasons – from a 'faulty batch of steel' to 'poor quality paint' – as to why this appears to be the case, but no official explanation has been forthcoming and it is most unlikely that one ever will. In any case, there are 1972 vehicles around in beautiful and original condition to test the validity of the theory, but it is mentioned in passing for the benefit of anyone who may be considering the purchase of a '72.

There were many other modifications made for

A 1972 Bus is generally a rusty Bus, but there are exceptions to every rule, as in the case of Luke Theochari's concours example. Note that the cab step is outside the body at this stage.

the 1973 model year, including new cab steps cleverly sited to be inside the vehicle when the doors were closed rather than being stuck outside. An improved steering box was fitted and the safety-inspired collapsible steering column gained a 'crack/bend' hinge. Except on the Pick-up, there was the option of a three-speed automatic gearbox, the braking performance was improved with thicker pads, and the front turn indicators were placed higher up on the front panel either side of the air-intake grilles.

Things really started hotting up for the '74 model year when in August 1973 the 1.7-litre engine was dropped in favour of a yet more powerful 1.8-litre version developing 68bhp at 4200rpm and offering a top speed of 79mph. Average fuel mileage dropped to 22mpg and the automatic version could only manage 76mph but the new power unit was more flexible and offered better torque characteristics across the rev range. Owners on both sides of the Atlantic at last reported that they didn't have to shift down a gear when a long hill approached because the pulling power of the engine was sufficient for the

vehicle to be kept in top gear.

You wouldn't expect the people at Hanover to be content with simply fitting a new engine for the new model year and they weren't. The 1.6-litre engine had its dynamo swapped for an alternator, the sliding side door was fitted with an automatic lock, headlamp washer units became available as an optional extra, and the petrol filler flap was dropped in favour of a lockable cap, the latter being easier to manufacture.

Nothing much happened in August 1974 as Volkswagen, like everyone else in the civilized world, was in a cautious post-oil-crisis mood. Add that to the fact that the Bug wasn't selling particularly well in North America and that the company was on the verge of launching other important models including the Golf/Rabbit, and the Bus had to take a back seat for a while. If Volkswagen's past history has taught us anything though, it's that the company has never ever been prepared to rest on its laurels (or its wooden spoons like the K70 saloon for that matter), and by August 1975 the 1.8-litre engine was enlarged to 2 litres.

With a bore and stroke of 94x71mm, the new engine's capacity worked out at 1970cc. It developed 70bhp at 4200 rpm with dual downdraught carburettors and a compression ratio of 7.3:1. The 1.6-litre

Introduced in August 1970, the dual-port 1600 engine develops 50bhp at 4000rpm, but despite this much needed power increase the Bus was still no road burner.

From left to right, a 1973 model, a '74 and a '75, and nothing to choose between them.

Despite appearances, VW salesmen were kept as busy as ever as the Bay-window neared the end of its development.

version, incidentally, continued to be fitted with a single carb. Apart from the new engine, other modifications included the fitment of a pressure regulator for the dual braking system, and thanks to stiffer rear suspension the payload rose to nearly a ton and a quarter, up from one ton.

Acknowledging the fact that the second generation Transporter was nearing the end of its development, the official brochure for 1976 made it clear that there was no point in carrying on with change for the sake of it and I can do no better than quote directly from that source; 'The VW Commercial has nothing new to offer. Which is precisely what makes it so remarkable. The way it stands, it has been tested, selected, driven and found acceptable over 4 million times to date.

'Sure - in all the years it has been around, it was worked on and improved on, again and again. But it was the same basic idea which was behind its success in the past 26 years. Which shows that we were right in sticking to it.'

By this time, Volkswagen's immortal air-cooled Bus had become a familiar sight all over the world. It wasn't in the same league as the Bug where sales figures were concerned, but you wouldn't expect it to be. Despite its austere origins and original purpose, the Bus had become a sophisticated animal indeed by the mid-1970s and was as modern in its fittings as any mid-range family saloon car.

By 1976, all models in the range were fitted with a

Crauford Matthews' Bus is driven all year round, has never been garaged, and despite having completed more than 100,000 miles regularly picks up top concours trophies.

*Graham Watson's immaculate 2-litre Devon Eurovette is a
restored 1975 example with a nose-mounted spare wheel,
optional chrome grille and over 100,000 miles to its credit.*

The ultimate Bay-window Bus, with four-wheel drive, but Volkswagen shelved the project after building just five prototypes.

good quality headliner, safety door handles and screw-type safety belt mountings for all the seats. Underseal was applied to the underbody and the driver's seat was fully adjustable in all directions, a feature which still isn't universal in the 1990s in the world of commercial vehicles.

On top of these small but nonetheless important points, there were dozens of optional extras available, whether you wanted to buy a straightforward Pick-up or a range-topping Bus. These included halogen headlights, laminated windscreen, heated rear window, dual reversing lights, automatic transmission on the 2-litre, safety padding for the instrument panel and even an automatically operated step below the sliding door. The list could go on and on, but the point is that if it had been invented, Volkswagen could probably offer it to you if you wanted it. The dozens of extras had to be paid for, of course, but it is typical of the company that they gave you the choice and – as usual – the range of items offered

as optional extras was very large.

For 1977 and 1978 things were left virtually the same, save that a special eight-seater 2-litre luxury Bus was offered in metallic silver for 1978. Although never marketed, Volkswagen's development department came up with five prototypes for a four-wheel-drive Bus in the same year. The now thriving four-wheel-drive leisure market was a long way off in the late 1970s but Volkswagen predicted correctly then that having two extra driven wheels would one day pay dividends.

In May 1979, after 30 years of Transporter production, Volkswagen announced its third-generation Bus which, with an all-new concept, would carry the company's commercial-vehicle banner through the 1980s and beyond.

Bay-window production ended in 1979 to make way for a new and wholly different model, but it is this 'box on wheels' that forms the backbone of the enthusiast's clubs today.

Mike Allen's 1979 Double-cap Pick-up (below) still has to work hard for a living but is maintained in tip-top condition.

Wedge Models 1979-82

Aerodynamic theory was put into practice with the third generation Transporters launched in 1979.

By the late 1970s aerodynamics were playing an increasingly important part in bodywork styling as more and more pressure was placed on manufacturers to build vehicles that used less fuel. As a science, aerodynamics was becoming better understood thanks to years of expensive research by theorists and technicians working at universities and in the world of motor sport.

Suddenly new words like 'drag-co-efficient', 'drag-factor' and 'Cd' were added to the already comprehensive technical vocabulary of the car-buying public, and anyone brave enough to engage in a pub conversation on the subject would soon learn in insufferable and horrible detail about the importance of 'reducing the frontal area', about why door mirrors gave bodywork stylists so many sleepless nights, about why windshield wipers should be hidden below the hood, and why everyone should rush out and buy the very latest wind-cheating automobile from the clever people who, at last, had come round to the same ideas laid down by Ferdinand Porsche 50 years previously.

When, in August 1979, Volkswagen launched the replacement for the Bay-window Bus, some of this new thinking was embodied in the concept and what loyal Transporter customers got was a wonderful Wedge. The engine was still in the right place for a vehicle of its type and the motor was still air-

cooled, but the body styling made a significant and welcome break from the past.

Whereas the Split-screen Bus was cute and pretty and the Bay-window was interesting and totally functional, the new third-generation Transporter was all of those rolled into one well thought out package. There were the same basic models as ever, of course, but in addition to giving a great deal more thought to improving interior space, the designers had to come up with several detail improvements across the board.

The large and elegant body, with its sloping nose and tail and swaged lines on the side panels, gave an overall impression of efficiency. Possibly without realising it, Volkswagen had created yet another classic. And this time, there was no doubt what generic name you gave to the vehicles. Up until this time, even dyed-in-the-wool enthusiasts disagreed about the correct appellation to bestow upon a Type 2. At the Volkswagen factory, everything was made under the name 'Transporter' when referring to the range as a whole. In America, most (but by no means all) folks called the Type 2 a Bus, but with the new Type 2 the goods vehicles became officially known as Transporters and the personnel carriers were called Buses – and both types were badged to that effect.

What we got was an improved version that had

The massive tailgate and large sliding side door further improved access to the Panelvan's load area.

The Wedge's larger sliding door also made life easier for passengers to climb aboard.

been increased in width by 5 inches and in length by 2½ inches, but the height remained the same to ensure access to garages and multi-storey car parks. The steeply raked windshield was enlarged by some 21 per cent, offering better forward visibility than ever before, and there was a new 'full width' grille high up in the front panel with the VW roundel placed centrally and also incorporating the head-lights. Wrap-round turn indicators were placed between the bumper and the headlights and the

bumpers themselves were of stronger construction.

The rear of the vehicle was completely reshaped, with a larger tailgate self-supported on gas-filled struts, and the rear window was almost doubled in size. The tail-light clusters were also to a completely fresh design and incorporated reversing and fog lamps. Open the tailgate and it was instantly appar-ent that more space had been 'found' by lowering the height of the rear platform - by as much as 5.7 inches – a move which increased the volume above the

Access to the engine was made easier with a lift-up lid in the rear luggage bay.

engine compartment by 40 per cent. The spare wheel was relocated in the front under the cab and the engine was now accessible through a removable hatch in the rear compartment, an arrangement employed on the Type 3 and 4 passenger saloons of yesteryear.

Like the very best ideas, the concept of the new Wedge was simple. There was nothing radical and no single aspect of the design broke new ground. The fact that access to the engine for servicing purposes could be gained through a lid in the top of the luggage compartment, as mentioned above, is a good example. It had been done before but when the idea was 'transferred' to the Bus and Transporter, life suddenly became very much easier for the mechanics working in the dealer network and elsewhere.

Installed below deck was a choice of either the 1.6-litre 50bhp engine or the powerful 2-litre 70bhp unit, both designed to run on 91 RON fuel. Four-speed manual transmission was standard on both models, and a 3-speed automatic was available on the 2-litre. Incidentally, the 1.6-litre engine underwent something of a slimming exercise so that the floor of the luggage compartment could be reduced

in height. The cooling fan was moved to the nose of the crankshaft and the fuel pump, air filter, alternator and distributor were repositioned at the sides of the engine, making for a very compact unit indeed.

The new Bus was available as an eight- or nine-seater with standard or 'L' trim, the 'L' standing for Luxury as usual. The L model had many special features such as brightwork on the front grille and windows, decorative stripes and two-tone paint schemes. In addition, there were chromed protection bars inside the rear doors, and the bumpers, which came with rubber inserts, were also chromium-plated.

Inside, the Bus L was fitted with wall-to-wall carpeting in the luggage compartment, there was a clock, a cigarette lighter, padded armrests, opening quarter lights in the front doors and much more besides. Pick-up, Panelvan, Double-cab and High-top versions were available as before, with a bewildering range of optional extras that differed according to the market in which they were purchased.

By the late 1970s and early '80s, Volkswagen faced strong competition in the commercial vehicle market, but the Pick-up continued to sell at a healthy pace. The 70bhp 2-litre version is capable of 90mph even with a load on board.

However, the most significant break with Volks-wagen tradition came in the form of a wholly revised suspension system. Out went the old torsion bars that had served so many different models so well for such a long time and in their place came an alto-gether more modern layout. At the front there were double wishbones and progressive coil springs, and at the rear there were semi-trailing arms with coil springs. Built into the centre of the rear springs were rubber 'miniblocks', which came into contact with pedestals mounted on the trailing arms to act as buffers when the springs bottomed out. Naturally, both front and rear had telescopic shock absorbers, and the front end suspension featured an anti-roll bar. The new system saved not only weight but also space, and the turning circle was reduced to around 10.5 metres/27feet. Not least of the novelties was rack-and-pinion steering.

Whether the purists approved or not, this was most definitely the way forward for future develop-ment. But, for the time being, at least the engine was still devoid of water jackets, hoses and a radiator. Not that there's anything wrong with water-cooled engines – it's just that when you get used to one way

of doing things it's sometimes hard to swallow radi-cal changes.

All the safety features of the old Bay-window model were carried naturally through to the new vehicle, including the impact-absorbing deforma-tion element behind the front bumper, front frame members that absorb and transmit forces to crumple zones, a collapsible steering column, door reinforce-ments and a roll bar.

During its final years of production, modifications to the Wedge were relatively few, for Volkswagen was paving the way for yet more modern vehicles with water-cooled engines. The classic air-cooled power units had served their purpose extremely well for many years but, to compete successfully in world markets in the 1980s, greater performance was required and that could not be easily achieved with air-cooling. A water-cooled 4-cylinder in-line 50bhp diesel engine was offered as an option in 1980

VW *TRANSPORTER*

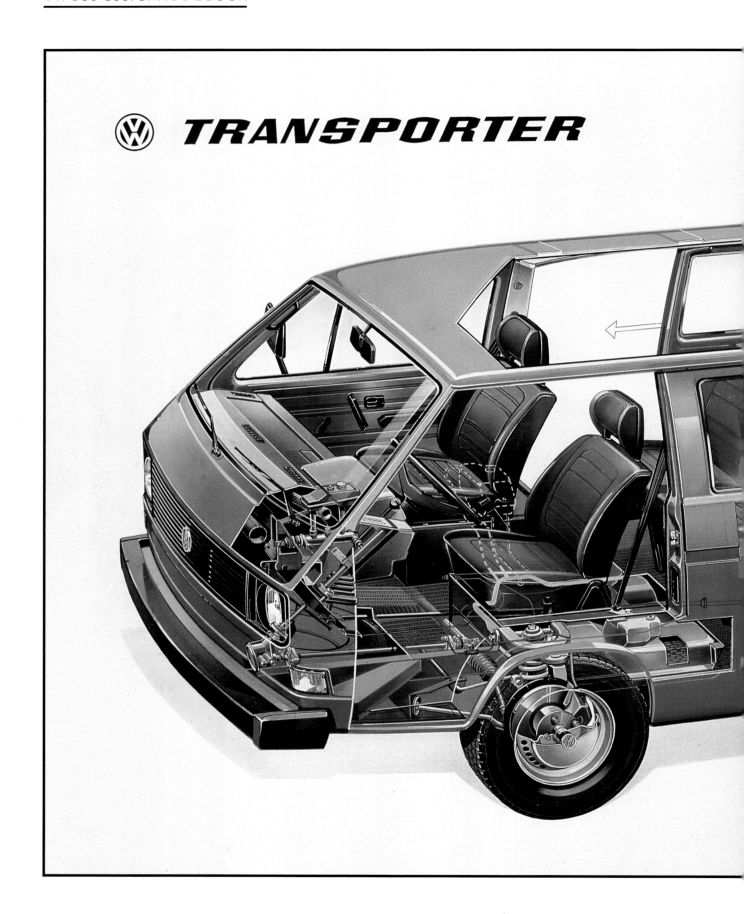

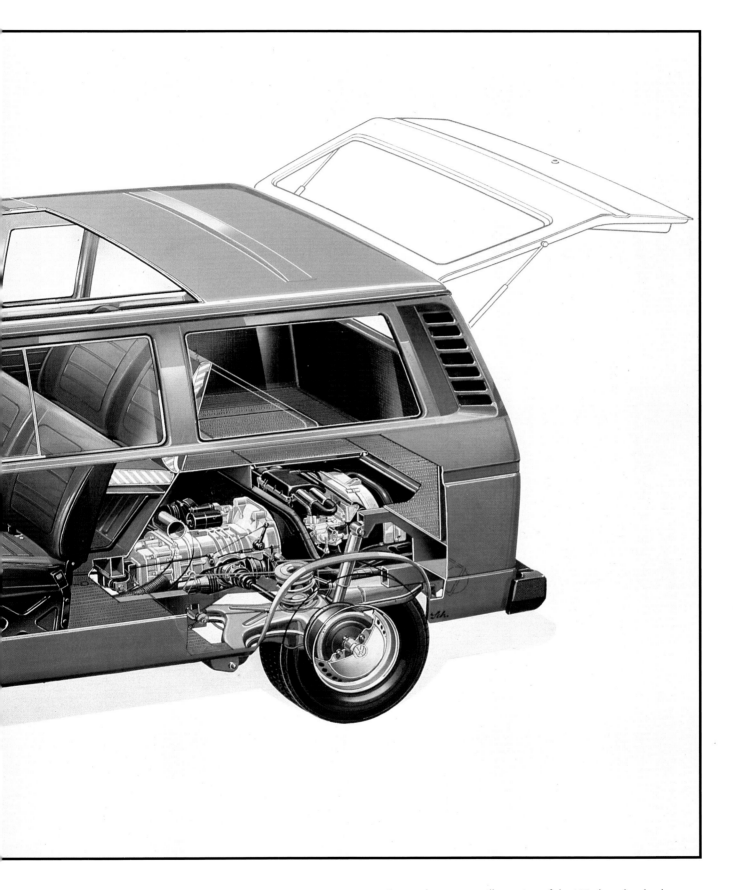

A superb cut-away illustration of the Wedge clearly shows the revised coil spring suspension which replaced the torsion bar layout patented by Dr Ferdinand Porsche in 1931.

Most sumptuous of the Hanover-made air-cooled Buses, the 1982 Caravelle came with a host of 'goodies' as standard fitments including a rear window wiper, additional soundproofing in the doors and tailgate and three-point automatic seat belts.

All professionally converted Camper versions are luxurious, sophisticated, thoughtfully and tastefully designed, but were far from cheap.

The Caravelle's interior is trimmed with high quality fabrics and wall-to-wall carpeting.

alongside the 1.6- and 2-litre air-cooled petrol units, a development which appealed to the increasingly large number of fans of 'oil burners'.

In 1982 Volkswagen launched a special Caravelle version of the Bus, and this was the most sumptuous of the people carriers ever made at Hanover. Additional soundproofing in all the doors and tailgate, trimmed window cranks, a foam-filled steering wheel, door and tailgate contact switches for the interior lighting and a heated rear window came as standard fitments along with a rear window wiper, three-point automatic seat belts and front head restraints. As luxurious as most high-spec saloon cars, the Caravelle had new and more comfortable seats fitted with armrests, and the headliner and sun visors were colour co-ordinated to match the rest of the interior. For some, it represented the very pinna-

cle of the air-cooled era. For others, it was time to mourn and to take up the challenge of preserving the past rather than looking to the future.

The last of the air-cooled 2-litre vehicles was made on July 30 1982 (chassis number 24C175000) and the last of the 1.6-litre Buses rolled off the assembly lines a few months later on December 31 (chassis number 24D051580). In 33 years, more than 4.8 million Buses of one kind and another had been made at both Wolfsburg and Hanover, a remarkable achievement by anyone's standards but no more of a success story than Volkswagen's customers had come to expect from one of the industrialized world's leading manufacturers.

With a growing family, Colin Rowberry made his own
luxury 'Caravelle' by restoring and converting a 1600cc
Panelvan for a few hundred pounds.

BUYING A TRANSPORTER

Most unrestored
Splitties and Bays are now in need of
major work. The body on this early 1960s example is riddled
with corrosion which means that the chassis is too, but an enthusiast prepared
for months of hard work need not be deterred.

Having decided that you can no longer live a meaningful life without an air-cooled Bus in the garage, where to go for the Bus of your dreams? First, face the facts in the cold light of day. Even the very newest air-cooled Bus is now over 12 years of age and the oldest are over 40.

If you're planning on buying one that is in need of a total restoration, it will cost you plenty and you will probably never get your money back if you sell it afterwards. You are going to buy a Bus because you want one and not as a 'blue-chip' investment, because even the very best original or restored examples are never going to reach dizzy heights in terms of price. A Bus is a Bus. It is not a Ferrari and it's not a highly-prized objet d'art. Few collectors and even fewer Volkswagen enthusiasts are going to pay

megabucks for a Pick-up truck no matter how many trick parts it's had lovingly built into its body and engine, no matter how long you've spent achieving the perfect paint finish and no matter whether it's capable of blowing off a Porsche turbo on the strip. From a basket case on a scrap heap to the very best show winners with their highly polished chrome and two-pack, we're talking sensible money. Which is good news for all Bus enthusiasts because it means that even the most impoverished among us can afford to buy something at least half decent.

Arguably the best place to start looking for a vehicle is in the classified columns of the specialist Volkswagen magazines, because this is where most enthusiasts are likely to advertise. They are also the most likely to have looked after their vehicles.

The local scrapyard is a good hunting ground for spare parts but beware the cost of restoring a vehicle that someone else has discarded. Without its cab doors and most of its seats, this Bus would be an expensive proposition.

Unless you are 100 per cent sure that the vehicle you want is correct for you, study the market for several months to get a feel of what is available and the prices being asked and, in the meantime, it will help you enormously to join a local or national Volkswagen club.

There are now hundreds of VW clubs around the world and all will have at least one or two members who are real experts and can help you in your quest. Attend several meetings and you will soon discover which people know what they are talking about. Good clubs usually pool their resources to help members, so when you need to borrow tools or even welding equipment the club can help. The richer the club, the easier your restoration work will be. Clubs are also a useful source of discount and inexpensive spare parts. Someone somewhere will always have the bits and pieces you're looking for, even if it might take some arm-twisting to persuade them to let them go.

Having spent several weeks or months listening and learning, you will soon become very knowledgeable, and the next step is to decide which model best suits your purposes. The pre-1968 Splitties are without doubt the most desirable but have drawbacks in that genuine replacement parts are more difficult to find and are therefore more expensive. In addition you will have to content yourself with 6-volt electrics.

With the earlier vehicles, you will also have to face the fact that the 1200 and 1500 engines are no road burners – great if you're never in a hurry but when you need to get a move on, the later 1600 or 2-litre will be a better bet. But if you are considering an engine tuning exercise you can ignore the fact that a '55 Split, for example, will rarely treat you to anything greater than a hardly-mind-blowing 60mph. But maybe 60mph is not a bad speed at which to

travel after all? Think about it now, make a decision and stick with it. Changing your mind after you've parted with your hard-earned cash could cost a lot more money in the long run.

It's rarely a bad idea to get a few views from other members of your family as well especially if you are planning on sharing your Bus with them. If your nearest and dearest would never be seen dead in a Pick-up or a Crewcab, you'd better change your plans now and go for something a little more comfortable, and don't forget that the colour of the paintwork is important to everyone except a dealer. The shiny lemon yellow Looker on the forecourt might suit you down to the ground but if your better half can't stand it, you're in for a rough time.

Anyhow, whatever decision you make, the next logical stage is to pick up the telephone and start answering the small ads. Sound out the vendor as much as you can about the particular vehicle he has for sale. He might live a long way away and nine times out of ten you'll have a wasted journey. It's not unusual to make in excess of 20 trips on one wild goose chase after another until the right Bus can be found, so don't be dispirited if you don't strike lucky first time. Incidentally, it pays to have a good pair of overalls and protective safety glasses before you inspect an old Type 2. You will be crawling amongst a lot of rust and grime so make it easy for yourself from the outset. And never be in too much of a hurry. The Transporter may be a light commercial but it is big, and there's an awful lot of it to inspect.

Be prepared for the worst and you won't be disappointed. A good many Transporters still in daily use – and the bulk of them are mid-'70s Bays – are in really ratty condition and not worth a second glance unless you are dead set on one and have the facilities to work on one properly. First, stand back and take a good hard look at the vehicle and ask yourself, does it look right? If so, move closer and start to be a little more critical. Talk to the vendor at length and discover whether he is a Volkswagen enthusiast. Find out if there is a service record available and whether the chassis and engine numbers tie up with those written on the registration document. If a reconditioned motor has been fitted you need to know who rebuilt it and you will want to know which parts have been replaced and which have not.

Next, it's time to check the condition of the bodywork and the chassis. In the case of a vehicle that has been restored it is wise to ask to see a photographic record of the work undertaken. Unfortunately there are dozens of ways of welding two or more pieces of metal together, but only the correct way will do for

Steve Saunders's 1965 Devon Caravette looks sound, but the visible corrosion on the bottoms of the doors, rear arches and quarter panels is hiding horrors underneath and the body is in need of complete restoration. Check out the back cover picture for the finished item.

the discerning owner of a Volkswagen. All too often I have looked at restored Transporters and wound up with the conclusion that the time and effort spent on such a bad job could have been put into doing a good one instead. Looking along the bodywork from front to rear, the panelwork is rippled with tell-tale signs of plastic filler badly applied, and in some cases the weld work is so bad that you can actually see joins through several layers of primer and paint. And the vehicle that has had a strip of matt black paint applied to its lower extremities is just about the screaming end. Naturally, all these faults can be rectified; in fact any fault on a Type 2 can be rectified, but at what cost to you?

Rust is a common enemy of the Type 2 and no part of the body or chassis is immune. Do not be fooled by a shining new paint job. It could well be hiding a host of dreadful horrors underneath. Wax polish is also pretty good at temporarily disguising scratches

Both rear quarter panels have rusted through from the inside, the engine lid is tatty and the bumper no longer sits straight, all of which will give you plenty of bargaining power when it comes to discussing money.

The valance behind the bumper and the front panel is particularly vulnerable to corrosion, and in this case all the sheet metal will have to be replaced.

It is worth inspecting as much of the interior as you can. Check the floor carefully and all the seam welds between the panels.

The rocker panel, jacking point and floor have completely disintegrated, but at least the damage is easy to spot and has not been concealed with botched repairs.

and even spots of rust, so look long and hard for evidence of blemishes under the surface, and don't be in too much of a hurry. There's a lot to look at.

Start at the front of the vehicle and work backwards. The front panel is inevitably the most vulnerable to corrosion because it is very large and takes everything that's thrown up at it from the road. Stone chippings will almost certainly have taken their toll here, not to mention the rust that will have eaten its way through from the inside. Replacing or repairing this panel is a long, complex job and should not be underestimated.

More serious than damage from stone chippings is rainwater causing rot from the inside out. The wheelarch panels, which are double-skinned and prone to rust, allow water to seep into the front of the vehicle and once the rust starts taking hold, which admittedly takes several years, it can and often does eat through the chassis sections. As far as is possible, this area should be checked very carefully indeed. Crawl underneath and take a good long look at everything with a torch.

The front wheelarches are naturally prone to rusting because they take a hammering from tarmac trash and the floor of the cab can, in time, quite easily disappear altogether. If you're inspecting a vehicle that is in a really bad state, watch out when you climb into the driver's seat. Your foot may well disappear right through the floor. While you're in the cab, check out the condition of the windshield pillars, especially at the bottom. Again, serious corrosion here means that the pillars will have to be replaced sooner rather than later.

Maybe the condition of the front seats is not important to you because you are planning to recover them anyway, but a well-used Transporter is unlikely to have been treated particularly well especially if it was once used strictly as a commercial vehicle. I mention this small point in passing because badly torn seats and worn rubber mats will add to the cost of any restoration work you may be considering.

The floor of the load area can also suffer from severe corrosion and where Camper vehicles are concerned, don't be fooled because the vehicle has apparently never had to cart heavy goods around. Over the years, the previous occupants of a Camper will have spilt drinks and all sorts of nasty things which will have almost certainly found their way under the carpets. In fact, over a long period of time, there is evidence to suggest that drinks spilled in the fuselage of a passenger airplane can cause corrosion in the airframe so it's a pretty sure bet that a Camper won't be immune.

Naturally the rocker panels are vulnerable. Rainwater and mud from both the front and rear wheel arches can, in time, find their way into the inner and outer rockers and cause havoc. Replacements are available and they're cheap but the inner ones are not especially easy to fit. Whilst you're having a poke around the rockers, you can take a look at the side doors, which rot along the bottom as do the front doors. New skins can be welded in but whereas with a Bug you only have two doors to worry about, you double the amount of work with a Bus. If you've got plenty of time on your hands though, why worry?

Another vulnerable area on Campers is the elevating or sunroof if one is fitted. Again, leaking rainwater will find its way through to the floor and rockers in some cases and rust is the final and inevitable result. Underneath the vehicle the chassis rails and outriggers are as tough as any you'll find anywhere but the elements will have almost certainly taken their toll. The main rails can actually crack in severe cases, usually at the point where they meet the outriggers, so check the whole lot very carefully indeed.

Both the torsion-bar suspension system fitted to Transporters up to 1979 and the wishbone arrangement of the last of the air-cooled vehicles are very strong and durable and rarely present problems. Torsion bars can snap, and you won't be in any doubt if one has, but it is more likely that the thick steel tubes in which they are encased will have corroded, sometimes very badly indeed. Take a good look everywhere you can. It's dark under there and holes caused by rust can be difficult to spot. And the same applies to the later vehicles, although a Type 2 made in the late '70s or early '80s shouldn't be showing too many problems yet. Leaking shock absorbers will have to be replaced but they're cheap and fitting them is comparatively easy.

If after crawling out from underneath, you are still in a fit state to continue and you haven't already lost your enthusiasm, the next point of inspection will be the rear quarter panels, which commonly bubble with rust for an extraordinarily long time before disappearing for good. Repair panels are readily available and they are easy to fit, so it's not the end of the world if they've gone.

You still want to buy a Bus? Good. Get up on the roof and check the rain guttering. Severe evidence of tinworm here is depressing because the little mites can cause large holes along the seams as they can with the Bug. Unless you really know what you're doing here, the repair of these areas is best left to experts. Only you can decide whether a vehicle in this state is worth pursuing further.

After thoroughly checking the above-mentioned points, it's not a bad idea to walk around the vehicle studying any area you think is worth studying. Look along all the panel seams for signs of rust breaking out, and check the window and door sealing rubbers. If they are badly perished, they will inevitably need replacing. Have you budgeted for the additional expense? If you want to keep the original

If the cab and side doors appear a little scruffy on the outside, this is often the true extent of the corrosion on the inside. With time and patience, this kind of rust damage is easily rectified if you have access to metal-cutting equipment and a Mig-welder.

Another common site for advanced corrosion, the side door post has rusted away at its base and will need cutting back before new metal can be welded in.

Rear quarter panels and arches usually rot in the same areas, and here the seam between the two panels has also started to corrode.

steering wheel is it still in good condition? If not, can you find a replacement that isn't worn? Small points indeed but they may be important to you.

If you are particularly interested in an older Split, also check the condition of those items which are now becoming difficult to replace. A good set of domed hubcaps, for example, is not easy to find these days. Yes, there are reproductions about, but in this author's experience not all of them have the same quality chromium plating as the originals. And the same applies to the headlamps, instruments and bumpers. Some Splits look neat without bumpers but if your plan is to retain them, check for rust pitting and chrome peeling. Re-chroming bumpers, particularly the American items with the additional bars that pass through the overriders, is an expensive business if done properly.

And don't forget the condition of the window glass. Here in Britain, a blemished windshield spells a definite MoT failure based on the supposition that a crack or a ding no matter how small or large may impair your vision of the road ahead. It's no hassle replacing the glass but again, it is important to budget for replacement items if they're needed. The overall condition of the bodywork should be your main consideration in buying a Type 2, or any vehicle for that matter. Good repairs are time consuming, and if you have to pay someone else to carry them out, expensive. If after your inspection, you reckon you've sized up what it's going to cost to repair the damage, then double the figure in your head because it will not take into account all the little items you've forgotten about. Don't believe me? Well, what about all those trips to the various parts suppliers, all those tools that you never knew you needed, the brushes, the paint, the thinners, welding rods, sheet metal, nuts and bolts, penetrating oil, gloves, goggles, the replacement windshield you just bought that your youngest son stepped on and broke just so you had to go back and get another, and new window winders? You know that you had a new set of winders somewhere but somehow, they just won't show up.

You can make a very long list of all the bits and pieces you need and it will never be complete. You're bound to have forgotten something and, when you get down to your local Volkswagen supplier, he's got a set of seats that look just that little bit better than the ones you have in the Bus at the moment. You can't afford them now but, maybe, if you save just a few weeks more, you will come back and get them. More expense again, so don't forget to double that figure in your head.

Mechanically, air-cooled Volkswagens are just about the most reliable and durable means of transport ever devised but that doesn't mean to say that even a Transporter will last for ever, especially if it has been neglected or abused. We've all heard it said

that air-cooled engines are living on borrowed time after they reach 70,000 miles but on the whole it's not true, and is most often said by people who have a financial interest in selling you a replacement engine.

An engine that has been driven sensibly (and by that, I don't mean one that has done 15,000 miles in 30 years or one that has never been taken over 40 mph) will last a very long time indeed if it has been serviced regularly and properly. We've all run Bugs and Buses way beyond their recommended service intervals and, to be fair, Volkswagens will put up with thin oil and wildly adjusted timing and cam followers for longer than conventional cars but, when the crunch does come, it's likely to be serious and expensive.

With that in mind, it is important to try and ascertain how the Bus you want to buy has been treated. Open the rear engine lid and take a look at what you see. Is there filth and grime everywhere? Are all the cooling trays properly in place? What about the generator pedestal? Is it corroded and likewise the rest of the alloy parts? Are the flexible hoses all in place? Does the carburation system leak petrol, especially after the engine is switched off?

Get a general picture for yourself and keep asking questions. Go for a ride in the passenger seat with the vendor before driving the vehicle yourself. Why? Because, if he's the sort of guy who shifts into top gear at 15mph (and I have known people who think that's perfectly normal) then you can safely assume that this particular Bus is mechanically as rough as a badger's backside.

There are many people who are just the opposite though. Because the engine is so far away from the driver in a Type 2, it's sometimes difficult to hear just how many revs you are piling on when shifting up through the 'box. Prolonged deafness in humans is therefore just as potentially destructive for the poor old flat-four as shifting into top gear before opening the garage doors.

Hope you kept your overalls on, because it's time to crawl back under the Bus for a look at the engine and gearbox. Don't be at all surprised if what you find is a congealed mass of old oil and mud, because the pushrod tubes notoriously leak on VW air-cooled engines. Most of us put up with it because stripping down the motor just to renew a small rubber seal that leaks a teaspoon of oil every 500 miles or so is perfectly acceptable. Serious leaks, though, aren't and a constant stream of the stuff may indicate that a flywheel oil seal has gone, in which case the engine will have to be removed and a new seal fitted.

Incidentally, a congealed mess is not necessarily indicative of an engine that is about to expire but it will tell you that the vehicle's owner can't be bothered with steam cleaning. Tidy methodical folks like steam cleaning engines and the majority of good

The body and chassis are in need of major surgery, but the grime-free engine has been well maintained and runs sweetly with nearly 200,000 miles under its belt. Watch for major oil leaks, worn bearings and a leaking carburettor.

Volkswagen specialists do it as a matter of course during a routine service. If the engine you are looking at really is filthy, draw your own conclusions. You will end up with more bargaining power when it comes to discussing money.

The gearbox can be checked at the same time, and the same rules inevitably apply. Evidence of a small amount of oil having leaked is not a big problem but common sense should tell you that gearbox cogwheels do not take kindly to being run without sufficient lubrication for long periods of time. Particularly vulnerable to leaks are the gaiters on the inner ends of the driveshafts which perish and split with age.

On Splits, it's also important to watch out for worn kingpins, the replacement of which is expensive and beyond the scope of most D-I-Y enthusiasts. The kingpin spindle parts will set you back the cost of a half-decent compact disc player. If grease hasn't regularly been applied to the nipples, the bearings dry out and everything wears rather quickly. If you do have to renew the kingpins, make sure that the job is done satisfactorily. You will want them to last you a very long time.

Most of the other mechanical problems that afflict

Transporters are common to all cars and commercials and can usually be discovered from behind the wheel out on the road, so remove those grime-caked overalls and climb aboard. First, check that you are comfortable up there. It's all too easy to blame the overall driving position if you're sitting on a badly-adjusted seat. Fire up the engine (from stone cold preferably) and listen for any unusual knocks or deep rumbling sounds. Don't let your friendly vendor try and talk over the noise of the engine, and if he turns on the radio straight away (or at all) be suspicious that he may be trying to cover up an unhealthy noise. All air-cooled engines will feel lumpy if it's a cold, damp day, but it shouldn't take long for everything to warm up so hold back for a couple of minutes and blip the throttle a couple of times.

Can you hear the exhaust blowing? Replacement heat exchangers aren't cheap. A deep grumbling sound may indicate excessive wear in the crankshaft bearings. Crankshaft endfloat should be checked, before and after a test drive, by taking hold of the crankshaft pulley wheel with both hands and rocking it backwards and forwards. If there is a detectable movement, it is safe to assume that the bearings are worn. For greater accuracy, endfloat should also be checked with a dial gauge. Firmly clamped to the engine, the small needle on the gauge can then be pushed against the pulley wheel to gain a reading. The maximum permitted tolerance is .003in. But with the engine running, it's not difficult to confuse worn bearings with a holed exhaust system. Take a good look at the latter when you've finished your test drive.

With the engine running, it is extremely difficult to know whether there are cracks in the cylinder heads. Sluggish performance is a good indicator that there may be a problem, but ideally, a compression test should be carried out on each cylinder by a Volkswagen technician. Blue smoke coming from the exhaust after starting the engine is the best pointer to wear in the valvegear but can be considered perfectly normal if the vehicle has been parked on a slope for any length of time. A constant stream of blue smoke will tell you that it's time for a complete engine overhaul. Watch carefully for the oil pressure and ignition warning lights. They should go out at roughly the same time. A flickering oil light may just mean that the switch is faulty – they often are on older vehicles.

Now select bottom gear, leaving the handbrake on, and momentarily release the clutch pedal. Does everything feel normal or does the shifter jump out of gear? If it does, the gearbox mountings may be badly worn or the problem may be with the 'box itself. Serious wear in the differential and crown wheel and pinion assembly will result in a loud and constant grinding or 'clonking' noise. Replacement parts are far from cheap and fitting them is not a job for the inexperienced. A secondhand or reconditioned gearbox is a better bet. Secondhand 'boxes are relatively inexpensive but fitting one will take a long time if you're a rookie to the job. Volkswagen clutches are notoriously durable, and in the absence of abuse, should last for 100,000 miles or more. A worn one, which will slip when it is engaged and send the engine revs soaring, is not at all difficult to replace but means that the engine will have to be removed to gain access to the clutch assembly. There are no shortcuts either, and although it is possible to change a clutch single-handed, it is better to enlist a helping pair of hands. Despite being made largely of alloy, the engine is very heavy and needs handling carefully to avoid dropping it on the ground and risking the possibility of cracking the crankcase.

Out on the road, you can listen for worn wheel bearings in particular but if you are able to satisfy yourself fairly quickly that there are no untoward noises, sit back and enjoy the test drive. A decent Type 2 should feel lively. The ride quality unladen is pretty good if a little bouncy over the bumps, but on the whole you will enjoy both the straightaways and the curves.

The handling and roadholding qualities of all Transporters are fairly neutral thanks to even weight distribution front and rear. On the limit, it is possible to induce oversteer but I wouldn't advise that you try on the public highway for two reasons. First, there is so little additional engine power to get you out of trouble if you need to and secondly, if you unwittingly overstep the limit and the tail end starts sliding at speed, the Transporter is so heavy that the chances of straightening it up again safely are minimal – so please don't get the idea that your new Bus can be treated like a Bug or a Porsche in the corners. In any case, it was never designed for racing.

Don't be afraid to stamp on the gas pedal a little harder than you might normally - it's important to check out the performance of the flat-four now rather than after you've written out a cheque. At the same time, you can test the steering for signs of sloppiness and the brakes for anchor power. Does the pedal feel nice and firm or is it spongy? Brakes and steering can be fixed if they are worn or faulty, but unless money is no object it is important to include all potential repairs in the overall budget. Remember, there are very few cars or commercials which have actually made money for their owners, even in the boom period of the late 1980s when prices for even quite mundane machinery rocketed. If you write down on paper what a vehicle costs from the time you acquire it to the time you sell it, there aren't too many people who can say that they have done especially well out of it. Motoring costs money, so don't get the idea that the Bus you buy for £500 and sell for £5,000 will have done you many financial favours. To get a Bus into a condition that commands £5,000 will probably cost you double that, so be warned and buy a Bus because you like Buses.

Having completed your test drive, you may have decided that this is the right vehicle for you. If it's not, tell the vendor politely that you do not wish to buy. It is not fair to walk away having told your man that you need time to think about it if in fact you have decided not to buy. If you don't want it, say so and you will be respected for your honesty.

If you really can't make up your mind, come back another day with a knowledgeable friend. Ask for the opinion of an engineer or a mechanic. He will probably and rightly charge you for his services but it's well worth the cost for a little peace of mind. A friendly member of your local VW club may be persuaded to accompany you. Listen to what he has to say. It may be wildly at odds with your opinion but in the end the final decision is down to you. Good luck and keep a cool head.

RESTORATION

Rebuilding your Bus

More than half the battle of carrying out any restoration work successfully is having the correct tools to hand and an uncluttered place in which to work. The other half of the equation is having sufficient patience to see the project through to the end. Take a look at the small ads in virtually any motoring magazine these days and you will find lots of vehicles for sale as an ' unfinished project due to lack of time'. Invariably, it is not lack of time at all that prevents well-meaning folks from rebuilding the cars of their dreams. Take a look in their garages and you will usually find piles of junk that has accumulated over 20 years or more. There's oil caked with mud on the floor, there's no power point for heating and lighting and you can hardly move from one end to the other for discarded garden tools. If you too want to end up with an 'unfinished project' which you will never be able to even sell, this is certainly the right way to go about it. What you want is just the opposite. You've just spent good money on a Bus for restoration so, don't throw it all away by starting like so many others. Firstly, clear out the garage and thoroughly clean the floor. Afterwards, assuming you have the will to continue, the next job is thoroughly cleaning the Bus. Remember all the pictures in the Volkswagen handbook that show you how to service your vehicle? All the nuts and bolts were beautifully clean and easy to get at, weren't they? And the instructions said things like, 'Use a 13mm spanner to loosen the nut.' Like me, you've probably wondered why, after following the instructions to the letter, nothing happened. The answer is that absolutely no-one can be expected to do a job satisfactorily if the vehicle in question is in a similar state to the average garage. There's mud and grime caked everywhere and in some cases, you can't even see the 13mm bolt you need to loosen let alone get a spanner on it.

Clean the Bus off thoroughly, on top, inside and underneath. If you have access to a steam cleaner for the underside, so much the better. If you haven't, it's a case of using a hose-pipe or a bucket of water and a sponge for hours on end to ensure that every last speck of grime has gone. There are a number of really good products on the market you can buy at any motor accessory shop that will help you relieve the underside of the Bus of old oil. Don't underestimate the time this stage might take. Cleaning off an old rusty vehicle is hard work and you're bound to be interrupted.

So, you got this far? Congratulations. Clear away all the dirt that's fallen off the Bus, brush away the water leaving everything nice and clean, and close the garage doors. Walk away from the whole lot and take a nice long break for as long as you like. In the meantime, think about what you want to do next and start compiling a list of the tools you'll need for the future. And remember that for every hour you work in the garage, you'll spend two thinking about it both before and after.

Start your restoration by thoroughly cleaning the Bus, stripping out the interior and removing all the glass. Removing the paint at this stage will make it easier to assess the extent of corrosion but a warm dry garage is needed to prevent the bodyshell from rusting further.

Do you want to keep your Bus in stock trim or are you going to tune and customize it? If you can't decide now, there's still plenty of time to make up your mind. So, on the assumption that your enthusiasm has returned, the next stage is to start stripping the vehicle down. If you're planning on a really full and thorough restoration, virtually everything that is removable will have to be removed so buy some sticky tape and a big bundle of loose-leafed paper.

Everything you remove will have to be labelled. Please believe me, you won't remember where half of the bits and pieces go when it comes to reassembling everything, and it's not a bad idea to take photographs as you go along as well. Photographs will not only help you to recognize the various components but will also serve as a good record of your work for both you and a prospective purchaser. New paintwork hides bad workmanship but if you have pictures that clearly illustrate your craftsmanship, it helps when it comes to discussing money.

Remove the seats, and all of the glass if you are contemplating a new paint job and store them away carefully. If the seats are in good condition, cover them with old bed sheets to protect them and store the windows as far away from children as possible, preferably high up on shelving. Glass can not only be dangerous, it is also expensive to replace if it gets broken. Another nasty job next I'm afraid; cleaning up all the old chocolate wrappers, coins, mouldy fruit, bits of chewing gum and car park tickets that have been kicking around the floorpan for years. You will be very lucky indeed if the previous owner hasn't kept a leaking oil can in the vehicle at some stage or other. Most will have and the result is one hell of a mess especially if the oil has mixed itself up with dog hairs and that awful fluff that always accumulates in such places too. A bucket of hot water, a hefty squirt of washing-up liquid and elbow grease are required for this job.

All the mechanical work on your Bus can wait till later because, right now, it's more important to get the bodywork and cosmetics right, so having cleaned the place up, take a good and long look at what you've got. Because it's nice and clean you can see every last hole and all that nasty rust. Ask one of your friendly club members to confirm that it's every bit as awful as you suspected it might be. A second opinion that is objective in its assessment will ensure that you do the job properly and don't cut corners.

Next, take stock of the tools you have and those that you are going to need. Decide whether you are brave enough to tackle the welding yourself. If you have never done any before, consider enrolling at a local technical college for a course on body restoration. The majority of courses are very popular but, if you're keen, get an application in as quickly as you can. You will be surprised how much it's possible to learn even in a short period of time.

Basic tools you will require include a power drill, a grinding tool for removing old rusty metal and 'sanding' down rough edges, a selection of hammers, a good pair of tin snips for cutting pieces of new steel, a selection of clamps for holding new panels in place and a bolster chisel. Welding equipment is up to you. Hiring the equipment may turn out cheaper than buying but involves a lot of hassle if you've got to make endless trips to and from the hire shop. Check out the cost versus the hassle and decide for yourself.

When it comes to welding, you've got more choices. Arc-welding is one that you can dismiss straight away for light body panel work although it may have its uses when it comes to repairs to the stronger chassis members. Oxy-acetylene welding is a possibility for use at home but the gas bottles are expensive and potentially dangerous in inexperienced hands. If you take the latter course, it is imperative to ensure that the equipment is stored well out of the way of curious children, troublesome youths and the sort of adults who constantly wear sticking plasters because they can't walk through the kitchen without falling over the kettle.

The majority of home restorers these days settle for Mig-welding because it's easier to use and the equipment is cheaper to buy. If you know one or two people in your VW club who are also about to embark on restoration work, why not club together and buy a Mig-welder between you? It's cheaper than hiring and you can learn from each other. Alternatively, look out for a secondhand set. There are some bargains to be had especially from the people who also advertise 'unfinished projects' for sale.

Now, you should be ready to go except for a few basic pieces of safety equipment. You must buy the best industrial safety goggles, the best and strongest gloves, a hat and a good set of overalls. And never be tempted to work, even for a second, without them. The potential risk to your health and the health of others is not worth it. Safety should be uppermost in your mind at all times which is why, before you start cutting and welding, the battery of your vehicle should be removed and stored well away from the work place. Similarly, it is important to drain the fuel tank completely and preferably remove it altogether, along with the gas bottles used for firing the cooker if you have a Camper. In fact all the equipment in a Camper Bus such as cupboards, wardrobes and the rest should be completely removed, because if any of it does catch fire you will have less than two minutes before the whole lot goes up in smoke. Standby fire extinguishers are a must at all times.

Whether you own a Split, a Bay or a Wedge, the construction is basically the same. They all rot in the virtually the same places, although as mentioned elsewhere very few Buses made after 1979 will need restoring yet. Whichever you have, you will need to buy repair panels. Independent retail outlets, specialist restorers and VW clubs are the best sources and every panel you are likely to need is available. Don't expect your local Volkswagen dealer to be able to supply you parts for Splits (or Bays for that matter) but every now and then a turnout of old stock will reveal that some dealers have been sitting on invaluable bits and pieces they never knew they

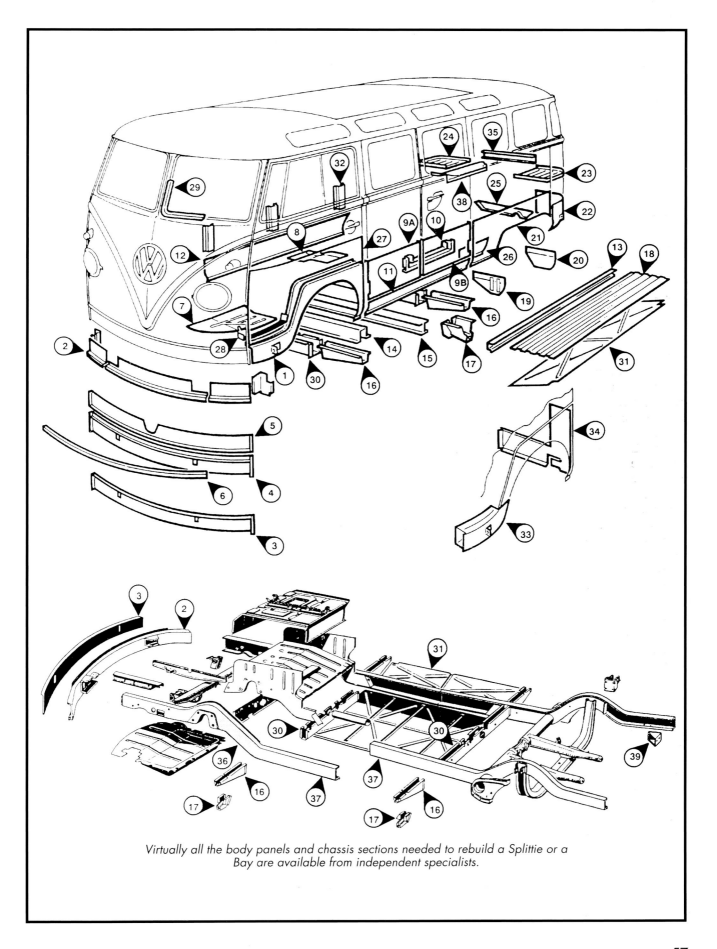

*Virtually all the body panels and chassis sections needed to rebuild a Splittie or a
Bay are available from independent specialists.*

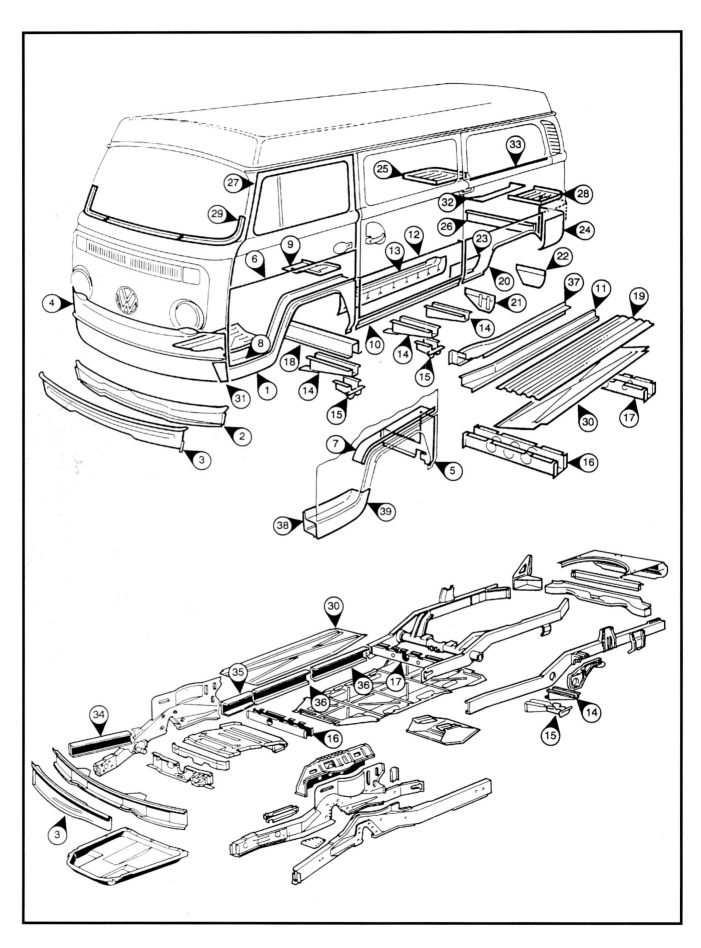

had. Keep your ears to the ground therefore for any dealer that is having a clearance sale.

Into the garage at last, and the first job is to remove the front bumper. Just undo the bolts. They'll come loose fairly easily. Now take a look at the front valance, which is the short panel situated behind the front bumper. Take out the headlights if you haven't done so already. Depressing isn't it? Rust everywhere and your first thought is, 'Who the hell let a lovely Bus like this get into such a terrible state?'

The answer is of course irrelevant, so take your power grinder or whichever tool you've chosen for cutting out rusty metal, and take out the valance. Once it has been removed, it will be possible to assess how badly corroded the curved box-section chassis member is that sits directly behind the valance. In most cases, it will have virtually rotted away and will need to be similarly removed and replaced. The front panel is a large one and it may well be that it is covered in large localized dents. Tapping them out from the inside is almost impossible because for the most part it is double-skinned. The easy solution is to literally cut out the dents and weld new sheet steel in their place.

Having cut out the rusty bits to your satisfaction, it is essential to tidy up the sharp metal that's left. A power grinder is perfect for this job if it is used carefully but don't be in too much of a hurry. One slip and you could cause yourself a lot more unnecessary work. Having trimmed back any 'excess' metal, use a hammer gently to straighten the panel which you intend to weld to. Any light surface rust left can be sanded off with an appropriate drill attachment. Ensuring that you've performed a good job at this stage will mean that the new panels will be easier to align later.

If everything's going well or not too well, take a break and carefully inspect your work so far. If it all looks straight and true, take your new panels and offer them up to the existing ones. The chances are that they won't quite fit properly. Replacement panels often don't, but usually a little fiddling around with a strategically-aimed hammer will soon have them shaping up. Again, take your time and offer up the new panel again, and if you are absolutely certain that it lines up properly, tack-weld it into place before completing the weld all the way across.

After it's cooled, the weld can be cleaned up with a grinder and skimmed over with body filler. Lead-loading is a better way of getting a perfectly smooth finish and it lasts longer but it is a skill which needs to be practised and is normally considered outside the scope of an average D-I-Y enthusiast. Lead-loading incidentally is also considerably more expensive.

Having completed this first stage you will inevitably have a lot of bare metal exposed to the air, which means that sooner rather than later it's going

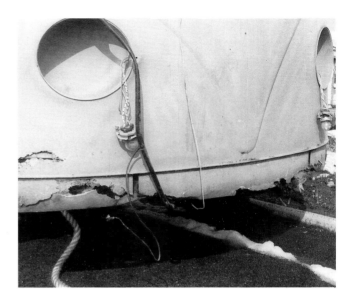

It is easier to work from the front to the rear. Here, the valance will need to be removed, but the corrosion in the front panel on the left can be cut out and a new piece of metal welded in.

The front panel is a large one, and because it is partially double-skinned, tapping out dings and dents from the inside is almost impossible. Replacing the entire panel is often the only sensible route but it needs to be carefully aligned before being welded into place.

to start going rusty again. If the atmosphere in which you are working is warm and dry and is likely to remain so for some time, you needn't worry about it too much but if it's not, it's a good idea to roughly paint over the exposed areas. It doesn't matter what it looks like for now as long as the metal is protected from rusting.

The windshield pillars may be in a bad state too. Tell-tale rust bubbles in the paint can be ground back to find out the truth. If there are serious holes, each pillar will need to come out, one side at a time, and new pieces carefully welded back in. Again, perfect alignment of the new pillar with the roof and front panel is vital if the windshield is going to fit properly again. By this stage, you will have realised that there are few secrets to bodywork repairs. Most of what lies ahead requires common sense, a steady hand and a great deal of patience.

If the wheelarches of your Bus are typical of the majority and haven't already been replaced they will have been almost eaten away, so it will be necessary to cut each arch away from the floor and front and rear side panels. The arches are best separated with a hand chisel. It's a laborious job and time-consuming too, but after welding in the new arches you will find it a great deal easier to replace the cab floorpans.

The cab floor comes in for a hammering on both sides of the panel, especially on commercial vehicles, but you may be lucky and get away with plating holes rather than welding in complete replacement pans. Incidentally, when working with the floor and arches, you will be confronted with a number of spot welds along seams which will require drilling out. And if that isn't possible because the flanges which hold one panel to the next are also badly rusted, use a grinder to cut back to clean metal and fabricate their replacements cut from new sheet steel.

There isn't much point in beating about the bush when the front arches have rotted to this extent, so the first thing to do is cut the arch away from the floor and rear side panel with a hand chisel.

After cutting off the rusty arch, the good metal to which it was attached will need to be tidied up carefully with a grinder and any light surface rust sanded down. A mobile sand blaster will do the job admirably.

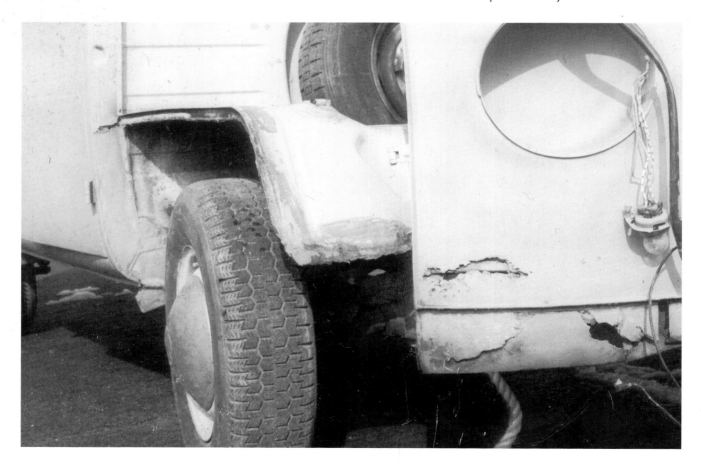

With the front arch removed, local repairs to the front door post are a good deal easier. A small area has been neatly welded here but will require smoothing off with filler or lead if the concours judges are to be impressed.

Sometimes it is only necessary to patch small holes in the cab floor, but this is a panel which comes in for a hammering on both sides and will need to be removed altogether in most cases. If the flanges to which it is spot welded are also badly corroded, they too will have to be cut back and replaced with metal. With the floor removed, the main chassis rail below can be inspected.

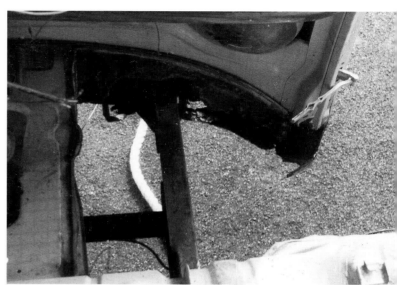

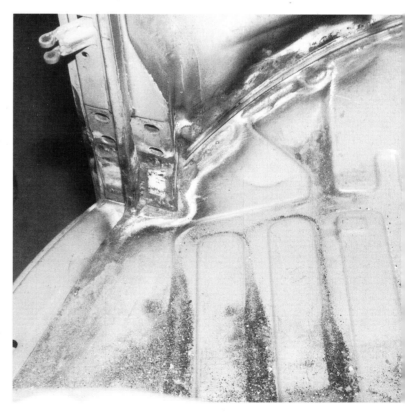

A new cab floorpan welded into place (above), and the bottom of the A-post repaired with a small plate.

There are no secrets to aligning and welding the front arch into place (left). The job merely requires a steady hand with the welder.

It all sounds complicated but the more you pull apart the easier it will be able to see how Volkswagen assembled the Bus in the first place, and provided you keep checking the alignment of your new panels before welding, you won't go far wrong.

The body rockers are about as straightforward as any ever are, but when you cut off the outer skins be prepared for another shock when you discover what's probably on the other side. Well, it's only rust of course, but it means that on both sides of the vehicle the inner rocker panels will have to be replaced as well as the outer ones. Before you cut anything out, check your new panels to see how much metal you need to leave and where, then cut out the old panels, clean up the area that's left and clamp the new panels firmly in place before welding. Again, do one side of the vehicle at a time. Get the rockers out of alignment and you've got problems, so take your time. These jobs cannot be done in five minutes even by experts with years of experience behind them.

If you've managed to get this far — and it may be several months down the road before you do — the rest is plain sailing because it's just more of the same. Replacing the floor in the load area is basically the same as replacing the cab floor except that there's a lot more of it, and repair of the rear wheel-arches and quarter panels is a matter of cutting back to clean metal, welding in the new panels and filling. No, of course it isn't quite as simple as that because every time you cut off one rusty panel you'll probably find another. You can go on and on replacing any number of panels, but in many cases it is possible to get away with sanding down lightly affected areas and treating with a good rust inhibitor before applying paint. It's up to you.

Where the main chassis sections are concerned, you may be lucky. Made from extremely sturdy pieces of steel, they take a long time to completely rust through, so it's often just a matter of cleaning them off and repainting them, but if there are serious rust problems, it's the same old story. One of Britain's leading Bus restorers, Alan H. Schofield, whose firm manufactures repair sections (for both body and chassis), reckons on welding one piece at a time to ensure that the body doesn't distort , and also recommends the use of a Mig-welder for the job. As someone who is considered amongst the very best in the world of Transporter restoration, his advice is probably best followed.

Bus doors usually rot along the bottom edges because the drain holes become blocked and won't therefore allow rainwater to escape. When you come to repair your doors, it is of paramount importance that you take your time in order to achieve a perfect result because you don't want to end up with doors that don't lie flush with the bodywork. If the bottom six inches or so have rotted, it's a simple matter of

Rot in the outer rocker panel quickly spreads upwards and outwards, necessitating the removal of a large area of rusty metal. Having cut out the old rocker, it is possible to find that the inner panel is also in an advanced state of corrosion and replacing both is a matter of cutting back to clean metal. After painting them, a generous and annual dose of Waxoyl will help to prevent rust returning.

The finished weld work to the rockers is neat and very strong but looks unsightly, so a skim of body filler will have to be applied before the Bus is ready for painting.

More often than not, the lower rear quarter panels happily rot away on their own, but here the whole of the rear corner has rusted through and the entire panel has had to be cut out.

cutting across the width of the door and welding a new panel back in but should the whole skin need replacing (panels are available), you will need to separate the two halves of the door.

A power grinder is probably the quickest and neatest tool for cutting round the flange although a bolster chisel is best used for the more delicate parts. Clean up the sharp metal surfaces, offer up the new skin to the main framework and clamp into place. Check your alignment time and again to make sure it's spot on and then tack-weld the skin into place. You will probably have to do a little hand work to get everything to fit properly before the final welding.

A replacement rear corner was salvaged from a scrapped 1962 model and welded to a new-old-stock lower quarter panel. The fit and welding are excellent but required some skilled handwork to ensure that the panels aligned with each other.

After cutting away the floor in the load area (left), the chassis rails are revealed. In all but exceptional cases they will have rotted badly and will have to be replaced.

There are so many body panels and chassis repair sections available these days that it is highly unlikely that you will need them all, unless of course your Bus is a complete basket case. If it is in a bad state, it is obviously important to be prepared for the worst and budget for it. One of the problems of restoring a vehicle as large as a Bus is simply that you can't see a lot of the corrosion damage, but once you've completed the welding to the underside, you certainly won't want to see all that new metalwork going rusty again.

Opinions differ as to the best way of protecting it from stone chippings, mud and rainwater once you've got it back on the street, but ultimately guarding against future rust problems once again comes down to the amount of money you want to spend. Many professional restorers these days coat all the metal surfaces with zinc, whilst others prefer stove enamelling. Rubber-based underseals have their uses but in the long run stone chippings will penetrate through to the metal, water will be retained between the underseal and the metal, and the rusting process will start over again.

Finnigan's Hammerite is an excellent product but you will need several coats to ensure that the metal is thoroughly covered because when the paint is applied, it forms small 'pin-pricks'. Finnigan's Waxoyl is also useful because, although it doesn't look especially pretty, it can be sprayed into all the nooks and crannies where it is impossible to use a paint brush. A thorough saturation in Waxoyl will have to be repeated every 12 months or so because it dries out and cracks. Old engine oil is excellent at repelling water but doesn't last long, is messy to use and is far from environment-friendly. Whatever method you choose, ensure that you use plenty and do the job thoroughly.

If you spend a weekend at a VW concours d'elegance you will see Bugs and Buses in the sort of condition that most of us can only dream about. There are restored and original vehicles that are 'better-than-new', and often their owners claim that, to maintain this incredible sparkle, all they do is keep them clean with a chamois leather and a duster. You don't need to believe them either because I most certainly do not. What the obsessive polishers never tell you is that they spend up to four hours every day with various and exotic cleaning materials peering into a nook here and a cranny there. Their garages cost them a fortune to heat all year and their wonderful Buses never come out unless the sun is shining. 'Use my Bus for a camping weekend? Never, I might get it dirty.' Well, each to his own, but with modern paints and rust-proofing techniques corrosion is not the problem today that it was when your Bus was new.

Like many other manufacturers years ago, Volkswagen took few precautions to prevent their products from rusting. You have just gone to extraordinary lengths to prevent yours from corroding, so don't think that because you've had to drive 300 miles in a thunderstorm that your pride and joy is going to fall to pieces because, it is not.

Having made your Bus structurally sound, it's now time to prepare it for painting, and as you have just spent a lot of time and money on body and chassis restoration, you will want to get the next stage absolutely right. The Transporter has a lot of bodywork to take care of, and what your Bus looks like after the top coats of colour have gone on will be all down to the preparation.

Getting rid of rust

No matter how much work you do with a sanding disc attached to an electric drill to grind out rust, you can never be certain of cleaning up a particular area of bodywork completely. Rust hides in microscopic 'pores' in the metalwork, and sooner or later it will bubble through the paint and spread to other parts of the body.

Taking steps to avoid this obviously makes a lot of sense. Dipping the whole bodyshell in a massive acid bath is one sure way of getting rid of rust but it has its drawbacks. One of them is that you're unlikely to find a specialist company with a bath big enough to take your Bus, and even if you do, when the Bus is removed from the bath you'll have to move pretty quickly to paint it before it starts rusting again.

The obvious alternative is to consider shot-, sand- or bead-blasting. If you have a local firm who can do the whole vehicle for you, all your problems are solved, but if you haven't, most plant hire firms can supply small sand-blasters which you can use at home. The machines are especially good for covering small and large areas and have the added advantage that once you've finished a rusty section you can slap paint on straight after.

One disadvantage of sand-blasting is that it can be very messy. It will be necessary to cover up all the mechanical components before you start including the engine, gearbox, brakes, hubs and driveshafts because sand is capable of entering every tiny crevice that you leave exposed to it.

Sand applied to rusty metal in large quantities under pressure and at high speed will get everywhere and because it is successful at getting rid of rust where you have otherwise failed, make sure that you wear protective goggles, gloves and clothing whilst the machine is turned on. And clean up the mess afterwards. It's not pleasant walking on a hundred pounds of sand spread liberally over the drive and in the kitchen.

Restoring the cab window frames is easier with sandblasting
equipment provided they are not completely rotten. The
rubber seals should be replaced as a matter of course.

With new paint, new rubber seals and the glass polished,
the window assemblies are as good as new.

Incidentally, if some of the body panels of your Bus have been badly affected by rust, bead- and shot-blasting will probably prove too powerful. Even sand might be in the worst cases, so if you do end up with a shell or part of a shell that is gone through in holes afterwards, I guess you had a pretty rotten Bus to start. Don't under-estimate the power of blasting and be careful how you go. Either way, the results should be spectacular.

For anyone on a tight budget without access to sand-blasting machinery or a large acid bath, getting rid of surface rust is not especially easy but can be done. Start by cleaning the rust away with an angle grinder or an abrasive wheel attached to a power drill and 'cut' the surface back to bright metal. Doing the same job by hand with abrasive paper and a wire brush is not only hard work but is also unlikely to rid the metal of every speck of rust but you're welcome to try if you don't have power tools.

After taking care to ensure that the metal is as 'clean' as you can make it, apply a good rust inhibitor and leave it for the specified time to enable it to work properly. This may take as long as 24 hours. Wash any excess off with lashings of clean water and apply a zinc-based primer. It is far from 'usual' practice, but a coat of fibreglass paste over the top followed by a thin coat of body filler is reck-oned by some D-I-Y enthusiasts to keep the dreaded tinworms at bay. Allow everything to dry properly and start flatting down with abrasive paper, after which, smooth the surface off with progressively finer wet-and-dry papers.

The next stage is to apply light coats of primer and again flat the surface down with wet-and-dry. When a satisfactory surface has been prepared, the top colour can be applied, one light coat at a time. After building up the surface, leave the paint to harden for three or four weeks before cutting it back with an abrasive polish and then apply several coats of wax.

When mixing body filler or fibreglass paste, it's a good idea to use an old ceramic tile because old paste can be easily scraped off. When using wet-and-dry paper, a few drops of household washing-up liquid in the water will prevent a build-up of sludge, and it also pays to change the water regularly. Another useful tip: when flatting down with wet-and-dry, use a rubber block inside the paper and move your hand sideways, not in the direction of your fingers. The latter will increase the likelihood of creating ridges in the surface of the paint which will show through after the colour coats are applied.

The above methods are useful for localized repairs but can be used for quite large areas if you have plenty of time.

Body filler has been applied over the welds where the rear arches and quarter panels have been fitted. Flatting the filler down at this stage is critical if the welds are not to show through the new paintwork.

With both rear corners satisfactorily repaired, it's time to get some paint on fast to protect the exposed metal. This is a rare high-roof split-window model.

Preparation and painting

It's your Bus so you can have it any colour or number of colours you like, but a friendly word of warning first. Vehicles put back to an original condition tend to command higher prices on the market than highly personalized ones. The choice is yours, and although you may be having a love affair with your Bus at the moment it may be all over in a couple of years' time.

To be candid, the correct thing to do next is strip the vehicle completely back to bare metal. You don't have to, but in the long run it's easier and by far the best way of achieving the right results. Chemical paint strippers are good for this job but, possessing the power to denude your Bus of its paint, they are not kind to eyes and skin, so carefully follow the instructions on the can and wear protective gloves, goggles and clothing. Nearly all paint products carry a degree of risk to health, some more so than others, and the same rules apply. Do not take unnecessary risks and keep all cans out of the reach of children and well-meaning but meddling adults.

As powerful as paint stripper undoubtedly is, you may experience problems in removing all the paint if your vehicle has at any time been treated to a respray. A few years ago, I restored a 1500 Bug I owned which a previous owner had repainted with a God-forsaken substance that just didn't want to come off. I applied one coat of stripper after another and absolutely nothing happened. I even warmed up one particularly stubborn door panel with a blow torch and still nothing happened until several fur-

ther coats of stripper were applied and the whole lot started to shift after violent coaxing with a scraping tool. If that happens to you, there's no easy solution and no short cuts (unless you know different, of course) so just persevere. You'll get there in the end. When the paint begins to bubble, scrape it off, and when you've finished the entire shell clean away the mess which, I assure you, will be considerable, then dispose of the 'peel' safely.

With the body down to the metal it's easier to see where the imperfections are, so the next job, if there are any small dents, is to fill them with a good quality body filler and really tiny dings with stopper. Allow each to harden and rub down with progressively finer abrasive papers. You might be surprised how many dings there are in what you thought were pretty straight body panels.

Stand at the front of the vehicle and with the light shining on the body take a long look across the metalwork. Every imperfection will soon be apparent. Don't be tempted to leave even the smallest because it will look ten times as large when the last of the colour coats is applied.

There are basically two choices when it comes to painting. You can use cellulose or two-pack. The latter produces by far the best result but contains isocyanate so do not attempt to use it at home unless you have the appropriate breathing equipment. Until two-pack paint has hardened on the bodywork it is potentially very dangerous, so it is best left to professional bodyshops. Regard two-pack as being outside the scope of even the most competent D-I-Y enthusiast. In any case, by doing all the welding yourself you've already saved yourself a lot of

Stripping a Bus back to bare metal is a long, arduous task. This roof panel has had a chemical stripper applied to the paint, and as soon as the old paint has bubbled up, it can be scraped away with a hand tool.

Painting in a confined space can be difficult and potentially dangerous, even with cellulose, so ensure that your garage is well ventilated and wear a clean face mask. Do not use 2-pack paint at home: it contains a deadly gas.

money, so why not splash out on a really excellent professional respray? Or spray at home with cellulose. It will take you a long time to get good results but you may consider it worthwhile. First, be under no illusion as to the size of a Transporter before you start. There are large panels to be covered and if you've never done any painting before you are bound to make mistakes. Not that that should necessarily discourage you, of course – even experts make mistakes.

Some of the common causes of problems include too much or too little air pressure in the spray gun, holding the gun too close to or too far from the bodywork when applying paint, a dusty or damp atmosphere, or applying cellulose on top of an existing paint surface with which it is incompatible. This won't occur if you've taken the shell down to the metal and can be prevented if you apply a coat of isolator paint to already-painted bodywork before your first primer coat.

Having made one of these classic mistakes, you are likely to end up with one of a wonderful variety of horrible paint finishes which will undoubtedly leave you in despair. But the beauty of using cellulose paints is that you can rub all the bodywork, or bad bits, down and start again. It's just more work.

First step is to acquire a spray gun and a compressor. Again, you can hire a set or borrow one from a VW club member. Someone is almost bound to have one. The primer, top coats and thinners usually come in tins, so follow the manufacturer's recommendations about safety to the letter. Cellulose is volatile and potentially dangerous, so ensure that your garage is well ventilated. Wear a protective mask when you use it along with the rest of your safety gear.

The general idea is to spray on one thin coat at a time in nice even strokes about 6-8 inches away from the surface. Lose concentration for a couple of seconds and you could find that you have put too much paint on one particular area, in which case, it will run in dribbles. This is bound to happen, so press on because each coat of primer and colour that's applied will have to be flatted off anyway. Runs merely increase the amount of flatting you'll have to do.

In practice, when runs occur, I usually try and cheat by wiping the paint off with a cloth while it's wet. Sometimes it works and sometimes the result is an even bigger mess. Anyhow, build up each coat and allow them to dry thoroughly between times. Exactly how many layers you put on is dependent upon the kind of finish you want, how much time you have and the amount of energy and enthusiasm you still possess in your body after flatting down with wet-and-dry abrasive papers between each coat.

Another thing that will try your patience to breaking point is the amount of dust that settles on the wet paint along with all the flies, spiders and other insects that are bound to crawl out of the woodwork

After several coats of primer, a colour 'guide' coat is applied to the High-roof van. Several more will be sprayed on top and flatted down between each coat before a satisfactory high-gloss finish is achieved.

When you have finished painting the exterior, there is still plenty to do inside. Maybe there is little need to take care in the quality of finish on the floorpans, but a prospective purchaser – not to mention concours judges – will be impressed if you do.

Painted to perfection: a gleaming Splittie dashboard ready to be refitted.

the moment you pull the trigger on the spray gun. There isn't a lot you can do about either of these problems in the absence of a proper spray booth, so be prepared to carefully rub down the paint after it's dried and wait for the perfect day for the final coats of paint.

What's a perfect day for painting? A nice dry one that's not too cold and not too warm and one when you feel fit and at peace with the world. A bad day for painting is a wet, windy one when you also feel stressed out, irritable and tired. The best results are achieved by those really annoying people who never seem to have problems, are always smiling and go to bed before 9pm. God, I hate them. Be patient when you're painting and you too will get excellent results.

Having finished the job, you will have to wait a considerable time to allow the paint to harden properly before polishing the surface to a mirror finish. Some people consider six months or more to be about right. Alternatively, it may have been more sensible to transport the entire vehicle to a professional paint shop in the first place for a dose of two-pack. It could be back at home within a couple of days, the paint nicely baked on and almost ready for its first shiny coat of wax. You would have saved yourself an awful lot of work and the results will probably be better as well. Two-pack is, in my opinion, the way to go but whichever you choose, good luck.

Now, with the body restored to health, it's time to put everything back together, and time for wondering why you didn't bother to label all the bits and pieces you took off your Bus.

Mechanical repairs should be left until after the bodywork restoration. Here, the engine has been removed and a replacement gearbox fitted.

A common problem on high-mileage Splitties: the bearings in the reduction gearboxes are shot and need replacing.

Personalization

Customizing the bodywork with a highly individualistic paint scheme is one way of making a Bus unique. It is a means of making a personal statement, and why not? With a vehicle as large as a VW Transporter there's almost endless scope for exploiting your artistic talents to the full.

Anthropologists have argued in the past that automotive customization is an extension of modern working class art which is born from an innate desire for body adornment. By that they mean bodies of all kinds, from the African tribesman who paints his face to perform a ritual dance, to Westerners who just can't stop themselves tearing their vehicles apart and dressing them up in a different set of clothes.

It doesn't matter whether the anthropologists are right or wrong because it is an oft-heard complaint that the cars and commercial vehicles which emerge from showrooms all look the same. The theory that everyday folks are increasingly looking for different ways of personalizing their vehicles is supported by a thriving, multi-million dollar industry specializing in 'after-market goodies' such as body kits, alloy wheels and the rest of the gear on sale in any well-stocked accessory store.

Spend a weekend walking round a Volkswagen enthusiasts' meeting and look at all the cars and Buses carefully. Of the 21 million Bugs and almost 5 million aircooled Transporters made worldwide, you will be extremely lucky to find two absolutely identical vehicles. I never have, and furthermore I've never driven two that feel the same on the road. The reasons are simple. No two are the same because all have been personalized in some way or other, even if the differences only amount to a couple of spotlights here and an additional head restraint there.

To the vast majority of people, the motor car is an

This two-tone Splittie is laden with goodies including a chin spoiler, spotlamps, chrome scripts, body graphics and spoked chrome wheels. The fact it isn't to everyone's taste is the whole point of personalization.

Colour-matching the wheels, bumpers and add-on chin spoiler to the bodywork (right) is an effective way of creating a head-turning Panelvan, especially when it is also fitted with a 1776cc 108bhp dual-port motor as this one is.

important extension of their personality and not, as is often claimed, a mere means of transport. The fact that you own an air-cooled Bus in the first place is an indication that you are probably different from the run-of-the-mill humanoid. That you have decided to restore an old Bus and make it different from anyone else's says something else altogether. Customizing your Bus for more power is discussed later, but while carrying out the body restoration it's important to think about and decide how the vehicle will eventually look.

Stock paint schemes look great, with a few notable exceptions, but with an infinite number of colours open to you, the aesthetics of your Bus can be significantly improved. Stripped of their chrome and other superfluous trim, the classic Cal-look Transporters, with their bright colours, lowered suspension and alloy wheels, turn a practical no-nonsense vehicle into a mobile work of art, but maybe you also want to go further and add a graphic design of your own to the bodywork?

Some of the quite fantastic designs and colour combinations which have been seen in recent years are the work of talented artists, but to achieve similar results you don't need to be an artist or particularly talented. All you need to do is make a picture of a Bus by tracing a simple outline from a photograph. With the use of a photocopier you can make as many drawings as you like. Then make your own designs using coloured felt tip pens or crayons.

If you keep everything simple it will be easier to transfer the design to the Bus later, but if you have the time there is no reason why it shouldn't be fairly intricate. Play around with hundreds of colour/graphics combinations if you like, and then make up your mind whether the end result is going to be a permanent fixture or whether you're likely to want to change it in the future. Thanks to modern technology, changing a design is easy provided it's not painted on.

Remember the sticky-back plastic so beloved of children's television presenters? Virtually every signwriter in the civilised world uses it today for doing the same job that was once performed with a skilled eye, a steady hand and a fine paintbrush. Signwriters and graphic designers use computerized machines nowadays to make company logos and designs of all types. Punch in the artwork on a screen, press one or two buttons and you get a print-out of what ever you want in any colour you like.

You then stick the design on the Bus and, if it doesn't look exactly as planned, peel it off and make a fresh one. Without sticky-back plastic, race car owners who depend on different sponsors from one meeting to another would be looking for a good pair of boots because to repaint one sponsor's corporate colours and logo by hand before the start of each race would be inconvenient to say the least. A word of warning though. Employ a designer or a signwriter to come up with something unique for your Bus and you will soon be adding plenty to your resto budget. Change your mind a few times and you'll be looking to sell the Bus just to pay the graphics bill.

Stop that thief

Car security is a big problem. During every second of each day, some idiot or other is busy stealing cars. It's an easy and lucrative business. The risks are low and the profits are immensely high. For the victims of vehicle theft, life is miserable. The months or even years spent restoring a beautiful Bus, not to mention the money it costs, can effectively disappear down the pan in seconds. In fact, it takes a competent car thief less time to break into a Bus and drive it away than it does to write this paragraph.

In the absence of agreed-value insurance, the money paid out by the insurance companies will never allow you to recoup what you've lost, and no amount of money will ever make up for the tender love and care you've lavished upon your pride and joy.

The major motor manufacturers are now working with security companies in a serious attempt to foil the efforts of car thieves by introducing electronic immobilizers to new models. Immobilizers are usually available as optional extras and work extraordinarily well, but they're expensive to buy and if, like the rest of us, you've spent your life savings on restoring and tuning your Bus, stretching to sophisticated electronic equipment is out of the question.

There's no single answer to making any vehicle 100 per cent secure from the prying eyes and tampering fingers of would-be car thieves, but it is possible to make life difficult for the thief and the various methods need not cost a lot either. The majority of thieves are opportunists. Very few will ever plan a pre-meditated raid on a garage and it is likely that, if they do, they will be after something a good deal more valuable than a Volkswagen Bus. If you can get a Ferrari or a Porsche for nothing, there's a vastly improved profit margin.

A burglar alarm fitted to both the Bus and the garage is essential but they have limitations. The noise an average alarm makes is pretty shocking but members of the general public are now so used to false alarms that few take any notice of them. An alarm set off by a burglar or by mistake is assumed to have gone off by mistake and in any case, the vast majority of folks don't want to get involved with criminals. Try and get witnesses to come forward after a crime has been committed and you will often find that you're on your own.

Six wheels on my Wagen. A 'stretched' Kemperink with two additional non-driven wheels.

It is obvious that when your Bus is not being used the doors, windows and engine lid should be locked, but despite the considerable risks, it is surprising how many people fail to take even these simple precautions. Leaving everything unlocked not only makes life easier for burglars, it may also affect a subsequent insurance claim. If you want to lose the Bus and the insurance money, just leave the doors and windows open.

In Europe, the huge amount of salt and grit deposited on the roads by local authorities forces many classic cars off the road for up to six months of the year. The classic Splittie or Bay gets laid up in the garage for the winter and thieves can potentially help themselves to what ever they want. They can and must be stopped, so what can you do to protect your vulnerable investment from going missing?

For a start, remove the battery and the rotor arm from the distributor. A thief may be able to find a replacement battery but a rotor arm that fits is an unlikely item in any thief's kitbag. Take off the expensive alloy wheels and store them separately in the house. If you haven't got a sufficient number of

axle stands on which to support the Bus whilst it's sitting in the garage, re-fit the original steel wheels and let down the tires. A Bus is difficult enough to push on to a waiting truck with its tires inflated let alone with them deflated – and a Bus with four flat tires doesn't look very pretty either.

It's tempting to cover up your Bus for the winter with a dust sheet or protective cover. This decision must be left to the individual but valuable objects covered up can invite curiosity. On the other hand, a Bus left out-of-sight is a Bus left out-of-mind. It's up to you.

There are a number of devices available from all good accessory stores these days which are invaluable in helping to deter burglars. If you have sufficient spare cash, invest in them all. The extending locks that fit around the steering wheel at one end and the clutch or brake pedal at the other are particularly useful and there are similar devices for securing the gearshift lever in place. A thief can obviously

A nose-mounted generator and smart alloy wheels certainly
make this Camper different.

A chequered flag – what more is there to be said?

saw through them but that takes time and the longer a burglar takes to steal his prize, the more likely he is to get caught.

Other less orthodox methods of deterrence which are effective, inexpensive and will give you increased peace of mind include 'blacking out' the headlights, windshield, rear view mirrors and tail lights. Use anything that's easy to clean off. Shoe polish will do the job reasonably well and not even the cleverest of thieves will be able see through a messy windshield. Vehicles driven at night without lights will also be more likely to attract attention from the police.

Coat every surface a thief is likely to touch with his hands in petroleum jelly or a similar substance. That includes the steering wheel, door handles and shift lever. It will not only annoy your man but, if he's not wearing gloves, you should get a good set of finger prints as well. Etch the licence plate number into all the windows and, in addition, it isn't a bad idea to mark the Bus with something which only you

know about and can identify. A special and unique mark on the underside of the chassis or anywhere else isn't a bad idea, but remember to take several photographs of whatever mark you make.

In fact, it makes sense to have a complete and comprehensive photographic record of the Bus which records every detail, especially those that make your vehicle unique. It is even worthwhile having additional sets of photos printed. Deposit one set with a trusty friend, one with your lawyer and another in a bank safebox. In the unhappy event of your Bus being stolen, your insurance company may ask for evidence that you took reasonable steps to protect your Bus from thieves. With a set of photographs, or even a video recording, you are strengthening your case.

There are literally dozens of ways in which it is possible to make life difficult for car thieves. No doubt you have your own ideas. Chaining the Bus to the floor, parking a car in front of the garage doors, dummy alarm boxes: they're all worth the effort.

DO NOT WASH!
THIS CAR IS UNDERGOING
A SCIENTIFIC DIRT TEST

R.T.T.S '93

VPA
703F

A seascape with snow-covered mountains (opposite) is appropriate for this High-roof van.

Fashionable scruffiness of the 1980s. Not all Buses need a high quality paint job to be noticed.

Smooth paint and body, lowered suspension, alloy wheels,
Stinger exhaust pipe and bumper removed – high fashion in
the 1990s for young Bus owners.

PERFORMANCE MODS

Unless you have as much money to spend as Porsche's competition department, it is important to realise that there are limits to tuning the business end of an air-cooled Bus. One of the most serious handicaps to making any Bus go faster is simply its shape. As people and goods transporters go, Volkswagen's products are no less aerodynamically sound than similar designs from other manufacturers, which means that when it comes to cutting a dash through the air, they're about as much use as a one-legged man at a backside-kicking contest.

Without a serious delving into the world of 'cut-and-shut' bodywork modifications, a Transporter equipped with a zillion horse-power is never going to be as quick as a Bug similarly kitted out, but that doesn't mean to say that improvements can't be made. How far you go is almost wholly dependent upon how much you want to spend, because having developed the engine, modifications will have to be made in other departments to make the vehicle handle properly and stop safely.

It is also important to take originality into consideration because the more tuning parts used, the less of a Volkswagen the Bus will become. If keeping your Bus original is not on your list of priorities, it's not a bad idea to carefully keep all the original bits and pieces in a safe place for the time being. They may well be needed one day, including the wheels and tires. Stock Bus wheels may not look pretty but they'll come in useful if some scoundrel jacks up your pride and joy and walks away with that sparkling set of alloy EMPIs.

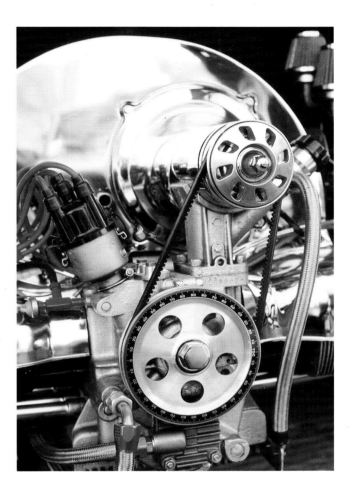

All dressed up and ready to go: a mildly tuned 1600 engine for street application fitted with a Bosch 009 distributor, a power crankshaft pulley, dual Weber carbs, and a Melling oil pump with feed to an external cooler via braided hose. The fan housing and cooling trays are stock but have been chromed.

Engine Tuning

Thanks to a number of mostly American firms who started tuning Volkswagen aircooled engines in the late 1950s and the 1960s, there are dozens of worthwhile bits and pieces which, if used in conjunction with each other, will improve the performance of a Bug or a Bus, but no single component will do very much on its own.

Designed for longevity and reliability rather than out-and-out performance, VW engines are the 'sensible shoes' of the motoring world. They will serve you extremely well and for a very long time pro-

vided they're looked after properly. The amount of fuel that finds its way into the combustion chambers at any one time is intentionally restricted and it follows that the rate at which the exhaust gases escape is also rather leisurely. Force the fuel in faster and get the exhaust gases out more quickly, and the Bus is automatically endowed with better performance.

But before driving off at high speed to your VW tuning specialist to spend a fortune on high-compression pistons, dual-carburettors, Superflo cylinder heads, a wild camshaft and a turbocharger, consider where all this tuning will lead you. If you use your Bus for everyday transportation, an all-singing all-dancing motor that develops an instant 400bhp as soon as you hit 4500rpm is not actually going to be a lot of use to you. Fine if you want to hit the quarter-mile in less than 12 seconds, and wonderful if you want to burn your tires away at the traffic lights, but the fuel consumption is going to be on the wicked side of sensible and any spare time you may have is going to be taken up with stripping the engine down and rebuilding it. Treat any vehicle like a racing car and, sooner rather than later, it is going to act like one.

The German company, Okrasa (now Oettinger) realised the exact problems involved in extracting greater power from the flat-four in the 1950s and marketed a complete engine kit for both the 30bhp and 34bhp engines which improved performance by about a third. Fundamentally, the Okrasa kit consisted of larger barrels and pistons, a heavy-duty long-stroke crankshaft with a 69.5mm stroke, dual 32 PICB Solex carburettors, and dual-port cylinder heads for improved breathing. Volkswagen continued with single-port cylinder heads for many years and it wasn't until 1970 that the company got around to producing an engine with two 'holes' in each head rather than one.

In America, EMPI likewise offered a number of tuning components including a longstroke crankshaft which, when used in conjunction with large-bore cylinder barrels and pistons (80mm) gave a total displacement of 1400cc. Denzel in Germany also made engine-tuning equipment including cylinder heads with increased size dual ports and, in Britain, Speedwell produced all sorts of goodies which no self-respecting boy racer growing up in the '60s could afford to be without.

Life in the late 1950s and the 60s for anyone with the desire to make a Bus or a Bug go faster was exciting. For example, superchargers made a big comeback and everyone just had to have a Judson, Shorrocks, MAG or Fageol 'Pepco'. The Judson was arguably the most popular and increased the manifold pressure by around 5psi at maximum revs. Supercharging was then considered a worthwhile, if slightly expensive, way of improving performance. The Judson simply bolted on and didn't require bodywork modifications to accommodate it, and a 'hooligan' with his foot flat on the boards could expect to have some fun. Paying for the performance was something else altogether, because fuel consumption suffered, and if peak revs were used all the time the loads imposed by the blower on a standard crankshaft and bearings were considerable.

Having been made by Volkswagen, the standard crankshafts, like all the other engine components, were over-engineered to accept overloading even for long periods, but when the crunch eventually came

it was going to cost plenty to put everything back together again. Old superchargers are now collectors' pieces and if you can find one in good condition, it won't be cheap. Still worth considering as a simple but effective answer to the question of improving performance, superchargers have two main drawbacks other than those already mentioned: firstly, they sap the engine of power to actually produce power, and secondly the additional heat produced needs to be expelled.

The rate at which heat is generated by an engine is directly proportional to the quantity of fuel used. Use maximum revs for prolonged periods and the cooling fan, which revolves at twice the speed of the crankshaft, can't cope. The answer to this problem is to not use the supercharger at high revs for prolonged periods. In other words, drive your Bus 'sensibly'. The increased acceleration will feel electrifying by comparison with that of a stock 1200 engine (expect an improvement of approximately 30 per cent) and the top speed will increase by between 10 and 15mph. Incidentally, a supercharger requires a separate lubrication system that usually takes the form of a small tank bolted in the engine bay with a gravity feed system to the blower. Naturally, it must not be allowed to run dry of oil.

The Judson supercharger fitted to this 30bhp 1200 Beetle engine was a neat way of increasing power in the 1950s and '60s, but there are easier ways of breathing life into the flat-four today.

In the early days, tuning a Volkswagen, whether it was a Bus or a Bug, was a comparatively primitive pastime. Here in Britain and on the European mainland, Okrasa parts were expensive and so was supercharging, and the majority of folks remained content with an extra carburettor and a Blue Bosch coil, whilst a very few lucky ones were able to afford the luxury of a Porsche 356 engine. In America, a number of far-sighted people took the business of tuning air-cooled Volkswagens a good deal more seriously, and over the past 35 years have developed each and every component to take a Volkswagen engine to its absolute limit. Gene Berg, who now runs a thriving business in Orange, California, started his love affair with the marque in 1956. At the time, there were virtually no tuning parts available in the States so, over a number of years he made his own. He reworked his own VW and was so successful that it wasn't long before a number of his friends asked if he would do the same for theirs. Wanting to make a VW go faster than a fire-breathing Ford or Chevy, Gene was one of those who fitted a 356 engine to his Bug at one stage, but he soon discovered that replacement parts were too expensive and concentrated instead on making parts purely for Volkswagen engines. Joe Vittone, owner of the original EMPI company, and Dean Lowry, Joe's research and development manager, all shared Gene Berg's interest in tuning VWs, and without them it is doubtful whether the VW tuning industry would exist today in such a successful form. Like Okrasa's original kit, products of the original EMPI company are much sought-after today by collectors who are prepared to pay serious quantities of money for them.

However, the heyday of tuning up stock 1200 engines was long ago, and things have moved on considerably since. If you own a Split-screen Bus fitted with a 25, 30 or 34bhp engine, there is a great deal that can be done to improve the performance figures but only if you personally consider it worthwhile. A replica Okrasa engine is a possibility and has the added advantage that although it can be tuned to give as much as 70-75bhp, it will still look like a standard Bus engine except for the dual carburettors and additional oil filter. But even replica Okrasa units are not cheap and there are easier ways of improving the performance of a 1200.

The first step is to dismantle the engine you have. With the engine stripped to its component parts and completely cleaned off, check the crankcase, crankshaft and camshaft for wear. An engine that has not had regular oil changes or one that has been abused over a long period of time will almost certainly show signs of wear in the main bearing saddles. If so, the crankcase will have to be line bored and oversize bearings will need to be fitted.

The pistons and barrels need to be checked for wear and the crankshaft for cracks. It pays to seek out the services of a good engine shop if you're planning any major work, although buying new parts may well turn out cheaper than machining and reconditioning old ones.

The 64mm crankshaft fitted to the 25 and 30bhp engines is not really suitable for performance tuning because high revs will ensure that sooner or later it will break. And even the cranks fitted to the 34bhp engines have only limited use. A later 69mm crank will fit in a 34bhp crankcase if you have any doubts about the original unit.

Rebuilding the bottom end of the engine carefully and balancing the weight of both the pistons and conrods to a fine tolerance is imperative in any tuned engine. Volkswagen's standard components are fairly well balanced to start with but if you're buying new pistons it will pay to ensure that they are within two or so grammes of each other. Get a set of pistons that are of exactly equal weight and the engine will be transformed, but only if everything else is OK. Polish the cylinder heads, fit larger-than-stock inlet valves, machine each head to raise the compression ratio, bolt on a dual-choke Weber carburettor and a free-flow exhaust system, lighten the flywheel by a few pounds, and you've got an engine that develops around 44bhp or the same as a stock 1500 single-port unit.

Was it worth it? Frankly, no. It would have been cheaper and easier to fit a reconditioned 1600 engine in the first instance, and for most road applications the 1600 dual-port is probably a good starting point from which to tune a Bus despite its propensity for cracking heads. If you already have one, how far do you want to go? Let's assume that your ambitions are modest and that you just want better performance for road use. The experience gained in building a mildly tuned motor may well provide you with inspiration to do greater things later, but for the time being let's stick to basics. The power output of a Bus engine is intentionally restricted in the interest of longevity and reliability, and if you keep everything nice and simple even a tuned engine will give many years of good service. If you want, it is possible to take one stage at a time without even removing the engine, so start with the exhaust system. There are literally dozens of after-market mufflers available and fitting one is just a matter of unbolting the stock system and offering up the new one. Don't expect a massive improvement in performance, maybe one or two bhp. If you are serious about developing extra power, it is important that a complete performance system should incorporate pipes of equal length running from the cylinder heads to the muffler. This will ensure that the exhaust gases are able to escape at equal pressure and will maximize exhaust efficiency.

The next stage is to improve the carburation system, which can be done either by replacing the main

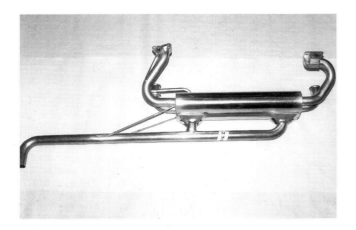

The Autocavan 'Powertorque' stainless steel exhaust can be bolted directly to a 1500 or 1600 engine and gives 2-3bhp over the stock system.

This version of the Autocavan 'Powertorque' exhaust, also in stainless steel, fits 1.7-, 1.8- and 2-litre engines and gives an increase of 4-5bhp without further engine modification.

jet with an adjustable one to improve the fuel flow or by fitting a dual-choke Weber in place of the stock Solex unit. Adjustable main running jets are not so readily available these days, but they still have their uses. To fit one, you need to remove the top of the carburettor and unscrew the jet inside. An adjustable jet, which is tapered into a seat, can then be screwed in to replace the stock Solex item. Setting one up to increase the fuel-flow to the correct degree is usually a long process of trial and error, so don't assume that you will get it right first time. In the long run, it is better to replace the carburettor altogether. The advantage of a single dual-choke carb is that one choke opens at a time. Potter around at 50mph in top gear and you're saving fuel. Put your foot on the loud pedal, the second choke opens, and instantly you have more power. It's a an effective way of improving acceleration without spending a fortune. Pay a visit to a local scrap yard and look around for an Alfa Romeo Alfasud – preferably one that is fitted with dual Weber or Dellorto carbs because you then have a choice of either fitting one and passing the other on to a friend or fitting both. Two dual-choke Webers or Dellortos will make a big difference to the performance of your Bus but only if the engine itself is substantially modified with a high-lift camshaft, larger valves and ports and a performance exhaust system. Simply bolting a large pair of carburettors to a stock or mildly tuned engine will merely increase your fuel bills. If you don't want to spend time looking for an old Alfasud a single 40IDF Weber or 40DRLA Dellorto purchased new from your local VW specialist will do very nicely indeed.

If you go for a single carb set-up, the stock manifold will have to be fitted with an adaptor plate, and if you decide to fit twin carburettors a new pair of manifolds will have to be fitted, along with a new linkage. Big carbs have a larger appetite for air and if

Stock dual Solex carbs are better than a single Solex and combine performance with economy, but their use is limited for tuning.

A single progressive dual-choke 28/36 Weber is an inexpensive starting point on the tuning ladder.

they are not fed properly you will have wasted your time. Therefore, fit a competition air cleaner and one that does the job efficiently.

The importance of a decent air cleaner on any type of performance engine cannot be overstated and if you've got a good one, look after it. That means keeping it clean and regularly changing the element whether it's made of paper or foam. It is so often the

A single Weber with dual 36mm chokes offers excellent performance for street use, but a brace is even better.

Good quality air cleaners are a necessary precaution against debris finding its way into the engine. This neat item, from a Kawasaki motorcycle, is one of four fitted to a pair of dual-choke Webers.

The Bosch 009 all-centrifugal distributor is the most popular of its type for tuning purposes.

Old Alfa Romeo Alfasuds are a rich source of performance carburettors. These dual-choke 36mm Dellortos can be used singly, with a suitably adapted manifold, or as a pair depending upon the performance required.

case that a malfunctioning engine is blamed on the carburettors when the real problem stems from an air cleaner that is either badly fitted or caked with grime. But don't be tempted to leave the cleaner off altogether. A highly polished alloy trumpet with a mesh gauze over the top looks wonderful but won't prevent anything much smaller than golf ball entering the engine.

So you've fitted a new exhaust system and carb. The next move is to install a Bosch 009 all-centrifugal distributor (without vacuum advance), which will improve the ignition advance system. Time it with a strobe to 28 degrees of advance at 3000rpm. Over advance and you've got problems, so if you haven't got a strobe, find someone who has.

Now we are getting somewhere, but of course

there is plenty more to do if you still find your old Bus is too slow. You should have noticed by this stage that forcing yourself into the garage to do tuning work is not quite as hard as when you were doing the body restoration so next remove the stock rocker assembly along with the pushrods, and replace them with high-ratio rockers and performance pushrods. High-ratio rockers simply open up the valves further than the stock rockers and allow a greater quantity of fuel/air mixture into the combustion chambers, which leads to an immediate increase in power. Performance rockers come in a variety of sizes but a 1.5:1 ratio is fine for everyday use. You will notice an immediate improvement in pulling power almost across the entire rev range.

The next stage is entirely optional and is largely dependent upon the climate in which you live. Fitting a small-diameter crankshaft pulley and a shorter fan belt will reduce the power used by the cooling fan but it also reduces its speed and thus its cooling efficiency. If you live in California and are planning trips into the desert your flat-four will need all the cool air it can get, so don't bother with a power pulley. If on the other hand you live in 'sunny' Britain go right ahead. Your engine will be glad to generate a little more heat especially during winter.

Because the Volkswagen engine is as dependent upon oil as it is on air to keep cool it is more important than ever with a tuned engine to keep the lubrication system clean and topped up. Regular oil changes carried out religiously at 3,000 miles will ensure long life for all the internal friction surfaces, and considering the cost of oil pushing your luck between changes just isn't worth it.

Over the years there has been much debate about the type of oil that should be used in an air-cooled Volkswagen. During the 1950s and '60s Volkswagen specified the use of monograde oils and dyed-in-the-wool enthusiasts swear by them today. There is nothing wrong with modern multigrades and it is doubtful that your VW engine will suffer as a result of their use. I personally favour multigrades because they're more easily obtainable but having driven many hundreds of thousands of miles using both types I can't honestly say that there is any detectable difference between them. If you are used to one kind of oil and you're satisfied with it stick to it. If you've bought a secondhand Bus that has always run with a multigrade, stick to it. Try not to chop and change: engines, like people, get used to a regular diet.

With a new exhaust, carbs, distributor, rockers and crank pulley in place, you've gone about as far as you can without removing the engine. At this stage, the Bus will feel very much improved and because everything has been kept in a mild state of tune, there is little need to start altering the brakes. The stock system will suffice for the time being.

If you want to go further, the engine will have to

Alloy rocker covers are not essential but help to dissipate heat more quickly than the stock steel items.

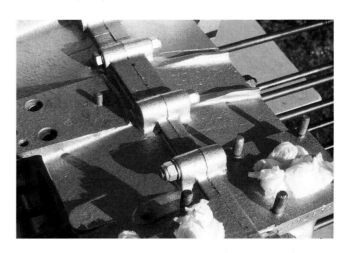

Whether stripping an engine down or building one up, it is important to keep everything clean. Tissue paper has been stuffed into the dynamo pedestal, petrol pump and distributor apertures to prevent foreign bodies entering the engine. Note the oil cooler mounting point on the left.

Volkswagen crankcases are tough and durable but must be checked thoroughly all over for signs of damage and wear. Hairline cracks in the face behind the flywheel are common on abused or high-mileage power units.

be removed, stripped and checked carefully for wear. Once you have the engine out on the workbench, dismantle it carefully, and religiously follow the instructions in a good workshop manual, preferably one published by the manufacturer. All the cylinder head and crankcase bolts need to be undone in a special order. Do not stray from it because when the engine is up and running again it will probably leak oil for ever if you do.

With the cylinder heads removed, it may be tempting to rework them and forget about the bottom end. An original crankshaft running its original bearings will not last long if all you do is restore and tune the top of the engine. So get the crankshaft tested at a machine shop for cracks, and measure up the journals to find out whether or not there is serious wear. Cast an eye over the bearing saddles in the crankcase for signs of scoring. On high mileage engines, or engines that have been allowed to run without sufficient oil for long periods, the crankshaft bearings can wear very quickly with the result that the crankcase saddles, in which the bearings sit, will be subjected to a constant hammering. The damage caused to the saddles can obviously vary and ranges from small indentations through score marks to complete destruction. If they are scored, the case will have to be line bored, and if the damage is really severe the case will have to be scrapped and a replacement found. Also, the con-rods will have to be checked to discover if they are still straight, and the camshaft will need to be measured for wear if you're planning on reusing it. If not, American-made Engle camshafts are a popular choice for tuning and they come in various sizes of lift and duration for different applications. The 110 is excellent for everyday use. Engle also make 120, 125 and 140 camshafts with various profiles that potentially offer greater performances but they are not suitable for road use.

Scan the outside and inside of both halves of the crankcase for signs of damage. An engine that has been abused for long periods or one that has been allowed to run with insufficient quantities of oil will bear all the classic signs of heat distortion. Fit the two halves together again. Do the faces meet exactly? If not, you've got a problem, and really bad examples may have to be scrapped.

Likewise, take a detailed look at the flywheel. With it detached from the crankshaft, spin it round to discover if it still runs true. Have it tested for cracks and check the friction surface. If in doubt about its health, replace it and have it 'shaved' for lightness, down to 13lbs, in the machine shop. At the same time, it is important to have the flywheel balanced.

Next, take a look at the cylinder heads. On high-mileage engines there's almost certainly going to be wear in the valve guides. Having experienced a dropped valve at high speed, my advice is, don't take a chance with the guides, the valves or the springs. Replace the whole lot. Stock valves are made to an exceptionally high standard, in two pieces. There is a risk of them snapping at the weld where the two pieces are joined together, especially on cylinder number 3 which usually runs hotter than the others. If you want to increase the valve size, go for 40mm inlets and 35.5mm exhausts. Any larger for everyday use and you could run into a few minor problems. Fuel consumption is just one of them. Inevitably, increasing the valve size will mean having to enlarge the valve seats accordingly, which is a job for a specialist and well outside the scope of D-I-Y at home.

One piece stainless steel valves are a good alternative to stock items and cost very little, especially if you only replace the four exhaust valves, but nimonic or titanium valves are infinitely better if money is no object. Beware the cost, particularly of titanium items. A set of eight will set you back the cost of a roadworthy Bay-window Bus, which is fine if you're planning quick quarter-miles but hardly necessary for the street. At the same time as you're fitting new valves, don't forget to upgrade the valve springs for heavy-duty items. Stock springs are OK up to a point but something more meaty will be needed for prolonged use of high revs.

Incidentally, if you have a 1500 single-port Bus, it is possible to bolt a pair of dual-port heads straight on to the existing barrels if you want. Single-port heads are not out of the question for tuning purposes but the dual-porters make life a lot easier because the latter allow more fuel/air mixture into the combustion chambers and enable the engine to breathe more efficiently. Whichever you choose, it is once again important to check them both carefully for cracks. The dual-port heads most commonly crack between the valve seats and spark plug. Don't expect to find a gaping great hole. A fine hairline crack is

After the carbon deposits have been cleaned off, the cylinder head can be checked for cracks, which most commonly occur between the sparking plug and the valve seat. Even a small hairline crack will mean that the head will have to be replaced.

about all you will see and the only practical solution is to replace the whole head. Sorry about that but not even Volkswagen engines last for ever.

The next job is to spend a little time with an electric grinding tool smoothing out the metal in the exhaust and inlet ports. Take your time and remove any burrs, 'lumps' or other imperfections in the metal, but do not polish it to a mirror finish. Matching the ports to both the inlet and exhaust manifolds should also be high on your list of priorities. This can be done by coating the surface of the manifold flanges with grease, 'Engineers' Blue' or similar. Bolt the manifolds to the heads and immediately remove them. An impression of the port will appear in the grease, and if it doesn't match up with the manifold apertures, machine either the ports or manifolds until they do.

Now decide whether you intend to increase the cubic capacity of the engine by fitting large-bore barrels and pistons. Going up a size or two is fine but large capacity barrels will require some machining to your existing cylinder heads and crankcase. A 1679cc engine is possible without machining the heads or crankcase, whether you have a 1500 single-port or a 1600 dual-port, but get to 1776 or 1835cc with a 69mm crankshaft and the crankcase and heads will have to be machined to fit the larger barrels. The amount of matching that has to be done depends on which size barrels you choose to fit. And whilst you're in the machine shop having these jobs done, it is as well to consider machining the heads for the purpose of increasing the compression ratio. Because of the reduced octane rating of modern-day fuels, it is not advisable to increase the compression ratio much beyond 8:1. Arguably the best way to increase the compression ratio is to have the cylinder heads machined, but by how much depends again, on the size of the barrel and piston kit chosen and on the type of heads fitted to your engine. And

there are complications because of minute discrepancies in the tolerances of the components in each engine. Before any machining can be carried out, the exact compression ratio of your engine will need to be established. The engine will, therefore, have to be tested by a qualified engineer for that purpose.

To increase the compression ratio on, for example, an 1835cc engine, it is probable that the cylinder heads will have to be machined by a maximum .004in, but if you ask 20 tuning experts for their opinion on head skimming for the purpose of raising the compression ratio, you are likely to get 20 different answers. The solution to this problem is to stick with your local, friendly tuning expert and listen carefully to what he has to say.

At the same time, it's most definitely a good idea to take advice about the use of unleaded fuels. It is conceivable that well before the end of this decade that leaded fuel will become a rare commodity, so maybe it's as well to convert the heads now. Some specialist companies already offer cylinder heads specially made to accept unleaded fuel. The extra expense is worth it in the end. For stock vehicles designed originally to run on regular leaded fuels, Volkswagen advise for certain models the use of five tanks of unleaded to one of leaded but it is not factory policy to encourage or advise on tuned engines. Common sense dictates that a power unit designed to run on leaded fuel should continue to receive a full-time diet of leaded fuel unless it has been specifically converted to run on unleaded. Converting an engine is not a job that can be done at home. The valve seats require hardening, specially hardened valves will have to be fitted and the compression ratio will have to be lowered.

Once you have all the bits and pieces together, all the machining has been done and you're satisfied that everything is clean, the job of reassembling the engine can commence. A qualified Volkswagen

With the valve guides removed, the combustion chambers have been bead-blasted and a small amount of metal around the guide bosses has been removed.

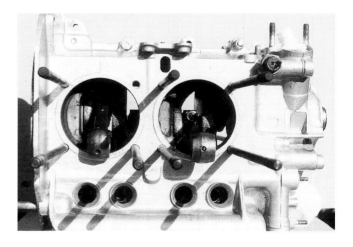

A stock 1500 crankcase can be used for barrels and pistons up to 1679cc but requires machining if you want to fit larger capacity cylinders.

mechanic with several years experience under his belt should be able to put an engine together in around four hours. Don't worry if it takes you a week. Bolting the crankcase together, fitting the barrels and pistons and the cylinder heads and finding there's something 'left over' is pretty distressing, so avoid rushing. In particular, take time fitting the gaskets and seals if you want to avoid irritating oil leaks.

Now you should have an engine that pushes out a healthy amount of power and one that will be enjoyable to use. Run it in properly, change the oil after the first 500 miles, and you should see it give really good service. Boot it hard from day one without giving everything a chance to 'bed in' and it will drop to pieces very quickly indeed.

As the later Buses came from the factory fitted with 1.7-, 1.8- and 2-litre engines, you may not consider tuning them for greater performance worthwhile, and you may well be right. For those who do, it is possible to go a whole lot further in the quest for more power. In fact, you can go to 2.4 litres and beyond if you wish, but the modifications needed will be considerably more extensive than the ones discussed above and your bank balance will come in for a hammering.

Before going on to building a really powerful engine, check with your insurance broker to see how it will affect your premiums. Insurance companies are not too keen on things like Weber carbs and hot cams, and you may not be either when you get a quotation. There isn't much point in going to the trouble and expense of building a fast Bus if you can't afford the insurance.

If you have one of the stock engines above 1.6

The stock oil pump (pictured) is adequate for mildly tuned engines but an uprated Melling pump is required for power units producing upwards of 65-70bhp.

litres, more power can be extracted by following the same path as we have just discussed for the 1600 unit. Polish and port the heads, balance the bottom end along with the pistons and con-rods, fit a performance exhaust system and a brace of Dellortos or Webers, and you're virtually there.

As you go further and further up the tuning ladder, you will have to pay greater attention to the engine's cooling system. Half a gallon of oil and a stock oil cooler perform an excellent job for mildly tuned engines but serious power generates masses of heat, and for the continued health of your vehicle it will need to be dissipated as quickly as it is generated. Without modifications your engine will at best run 'hot' and burn its valves and at worst will melt. By all means retain the small-diameter performance crank pulley and the stock cooling blower but some thought will have to be given to the oil system. Initially the stock oil pump will have to be replaced by an uprated unit. A Melling pump is as good as any (the gears are 38 per cent larger than stock) and will ensure that the oil is pumped around the engine at sufficient pressure when higher performance is called for.

The next stage is to fit an external oil cooler and a conventional filter. Ideally, the cooler should be placed well out in the air stream but at the same time well protected from road debris. Fitting it at the front of the Bus is great for cooling but has the disadvantage that exceptionally long pipes will have to be run from the engine down the entire length of the chassis, where they will be exposed to the road.

In any case, it's not a good idea to locate the cooler anywhere that requires the feed and return pipes to be of great length because lots more oil will be required to fill them. There is nothing inherently wrong with that save that it will require an extra large sump oil tank bolted to the bottom of the crankcase which will become particularly vulnerable if you are planning on lowering the suspension of the Bus. Why not compromise and place the cooler on the side of the bodywork just around the corner from the rear light and shroud it with a piece of aluminium? It may not look pretty but at least it will be out in the airstream and the feed pipes will be kept to a minimal length. In that way, an additional sump tank need not be too large, which means it will be less vulnerable if and when you lower the suspension.

To uprate the stock oil system, some modifications will have to be made to the crankcase, and that means a trip to the machine shop for a spot of drilling and tapping. To fit the oil pipes, you will need to gain access to the oil flow for the purpose of 'outlet and return' but, having done that, it is necessary to blank off the lower main gallery so that the oil runs into the modified system rather than continuing on its way as normal. It is preferable to use

Protected by an aluminium shroud, the most convenient position for an external oil cooler is a few inches above the rear quarter panel.

braided hose for the piping rather than rubber for the simple reason that the former is a great deal stronger. You can't afford to take any risks with hoses flying off or bursting under pressure so buy the best. The outlet pipe should run directly to an oil filter mounted in a position which makes it readily accessible for swift changes. It is often the case that a separate filter can become almost impossible to remove by hand when the time comes and it will, therefore, require brutal treatment with a screwdriver. So don't put the filter in a 'tight' space.

Ideally the oil line should incorporate a thermostat between the filter and the cooler to ensure that the oil does not pass through the cooler until it has reached a certain temperature. When the engine is up to operating temperature and the oil has reached a temperature of 70-80°C, a small valve in the thermostat will open to allow it to enter the cooler mounted on the outside of the bodywork. From the cooler, the oil is then returned to the rear of the crankcase to lubricate the engine in the normal way.

Lastly, where the oil system is concerned, it is advisable to fit a windage tray if you're planning on using your Bus for drag racing or other forms of motor sport. A windage tray, which is a metal baffle, fits below the camshaft and helps to prevent oil surge.

As for uprating the engine, you could go on almost for ever making improvements. With a really high-performance unit, it is necessary to consider a stroker crankshaft, full-race or performance con-rods, and the rest. The main objective in using a stroker crank is to increase the piston throw, or the distance by which the pistons move up and down in the cylinders. But because stock Volkswagen crankcases were designed to accept a 69mm throw crankshaft, fitting an 'aftermarket' crankshaft with, for example, a 74, 78, 82 or 84mm throw will require some machining of the crankcase to gain sufficient clearance for the con-rods.

Much stronger than a stock unit, a counterweighted stroker crankshaft is required for a large capacity high-performance engine but is not cheap.

As a result of increasing the stroke, it is also necessary to consider fitting longer cylinder barrels and shorter pistons as the latter will otherwise meet the cylinder head and cause serious damage. Again, the services of a tuning expert should be enlisted for these delicate operations because mistakes will be expensive to rectify. Correspondingly lengthened pushrods will also have to be fitted but the stock pushrod tubes can be made to fit simply by stretching the corrugated ends.

Having reached this stage of tuning, even more power can be extracted by fitting larger carbs. Dual 44IDF or 48IDA Webers are popular choices for engines above 2 litres, but although your Bus will be an extremely potent machine with either of these set-ups, fuel mileage will suffer.

As mentioned earlier, the length to which you go in tuning your Bus depends on what application you have in mind. For street use, it is as well to keep drivability on your list of priorities. A 2.4-litre engine that develops 170 bhp is fine if that's what you're aiming for but don't expect it to last for 100,000 trouble-free miles or offer you 27mpg because it will do neither. Fit a 'wild' cam to such an engine and it won't be especially pleasant to drive legally anywhere.

The aim of any Bus owner looking for more power should be to make reasonable rather than outrageous gains because the shape of the bodywork is going to limit top-end performance irrespective of how many 'ponies' are put to work under the engine lid. Ultimately, a Bus does not make an ideal race car — not that I would want to discourage anyone from taking a trip up the strip with a Transporter. Quite the opposite in fact, but it is as well to be aware of the very real limitations imposed by 'brick-like' aerodynamics.

One route to more power is to scrap the idea of using any form of Volkswagen engine and instead fit a 6-cylinder Porsche or Corvair unit along with a five-speed transaxle. This type of transplant should

The 2-litre Ford Pinto engine is a popular conversion but its installation requires bodywork modifications plus a special adaptor plate to mate the unit to the gearbox. Some prefer a Porsche flat-six, Rover V8 or Fiat twin-cam.

For large capacity engines up to 2.4 litres, the Volkswagen Type 4 saloon engine provides a good base unit, as its crankcase is stronger and the reworked oilways provide improved lubrication. Note that the crank-mounted cooling fan also makes for a more compact unit.

also involve fitting Porsche brakes and uprating the suspension accordingly, but be under no illusions as to the cost of Porsche motoring. It is not cheap, so stick to tried and tested methods and you won't go too far wrong.

Whether you own a Split-screen, a Bay-window or a Wedge, there's plenty of scope for tuning. All the air-cooled engines share the same design principles and if you don't want to go to the trouble and expense of removing, dismantling and rebuilding an engine for out-and-out performance, stick to the basics discussed at the beginning of this chapter. You will soon notice the difference.

A reworked 2-litre Type 4 engine (right) with a 'four-prong' Monza exhaust system sounds great and goes well, and with a perspex engine lid, everyone can see the results of your hard work.

Suspension lowering

Lowering the suspension can improve the roadholding and the overall look, especially when a smart set of Porsche alloys is also fitted.

Reducing the ride height of a stock Bus is not only a means of enhancing the vehicle's overall aesthetic appeal but can also improve the roadholding and handling. Finish off the effect with a smart set of alloy wheels and some decent rubber and even a tatty old Bus will look like a million dollars. There are however a couple of disadvantages to dropping a Bus on the floor which ought to be considered beforehand.

A really low Bus is not going to give you much ground clearance and if you're planning a camping

holiday off-road, the vehicle's undercarriage is going to take a hammering. Secondly, one of the great advantages of a stock Bus is that it offers such a commanding view of the road ahead. Sitting so high up, the driver can easily see what's around the next corner. Drop the Bus on its belly and that particular benefit will disappear.

Basically, there are three methods by which a Splittie or a Bay can be lowered. The simplest way is to remove a number of torsion leaves from the front axle, but please don't be tempted to because it is potentially very dangerous: one exception to the general rule that 'basic is best'. Removing the torsion springs will not only lead to a fairly 'choppy' ride but the overall suspension strength will be weakened, so leave that particular tweak well alone.

Arguably the most popular method is to drill the 'dimples' that retain the centre clamp section for the torsion springs, cut both tubes either side of the clamping section, set the ride height as required (with the Bus lifted on a trolley jack) and weld the centre sections back into position. To do this it is necessary to unbolt the front beam, remove it from the vehicle altogether and dismantle it down to the bare torsion-bar tubes. Cut off the steering pivot box on the bottom tube with an angle grinder. The assembly in the middle of the bottom tube that holds the leaves together also needs to be cut clean out so that the tube can be rotated. Half an inch rotation will give you a fairly sensible degree of lowering whereas an inch is fairly wild. Weld the tube back together and do the same on the top tube. Then, the pivot box can be welded back on and the beam reassembled. A competent D-I-Y mechanic will take a day to perform this neat operation. If you are considering drastic lowering, it will be obviously necessary to fit a pair of shorter-than-stock shocks and, at the same time, it is as well to check that you don't fall foul of the rules and regulations relating to the height of the headlights. The laws differ from country to country so, be aware of them before you start.

Incidentally, if you own a Splittie, you may like to consider swapping the stock king/link-pin front beam for a later balljoint beam. As mentioned elsewhere, replacing king-pins is expensive and cannot be done at home. Replacing worn balljoints is not only easy but is a great deal cheaper too, and a later beam will bolt on to the front end of a Splittie without the need to make modifications. Find yourself a post-1970 beam and you get yourself a pair of disc brakes as well. If, however, you are sure that your original kings and links are in good condition, it's probably better to retain them.

Arguably, the best method of lowering the front end of a Bus is to fit an Albatross Adjuster, a neat and adjustable device made by Bus Boys Inc. of Redding, California, and available through a variety of independent outlets. The Albatross can be used for lowering or raising the ride height and comes as a kit with a full set of fitting instructions. It's a fairly complex process but is increasingly popular.

Lowering the tail-end of a Bus is usually a good deal easier than lowering the front, and although there are differences in the layout between Splitties and Bays, the design principle of the two is virtually the same. Whereas with the pre-'67 vehicles, the rear suspension is a pure Bus swing axle arrangement, the post-'67 Bays are fitted with two constant-veloc-

The most popular method of lowering the suspension is by drilling the 'dimples' that retain the centre section of the torsion springs, cutting both tubes either side of the clamping section, setting the ride height by rotating the tubes and welding the centre section back together again.

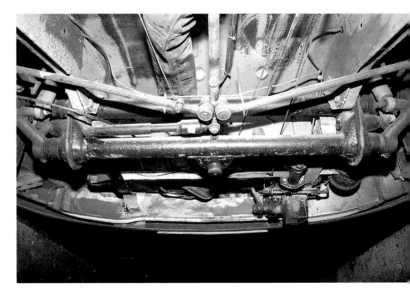

In this case, the front beam has been welded back together so well that it is almost impossible to see the joins.

ity joints on each of the two driveshafts to allow for safer handling by minimizing the possibility of wheel 'tuck-in'.

This does not mean however that the good old swing-axles fitted to the Split-screens are unsafe. In fact, anyone who actually experiences a rear wheel tucking under in a Splittie is probably on the run from the men in white coats anyway. It is of course possible to convert the rear end of a Split-screen to the later specification by simply installing a transaxle from a later Bus or a 1303S Bug, but there's no need to get the idea that because you've got solid, un-jointed swing-axles you've got to rush out and spend a lot of money getting rid of them. It just isn't necessary even if you have a powerful engine and, if you do retain the original axles, you won't have to keep replacing constant-velocity joints.

So, support the Bus on a good pair of axle stands and remove the wheels. If the suspension is covered in mud, wash it off straight away before it starts flaking all over your hands and tools and then mark off a reference point between the hub assembly and the spring plate with a piece of chalk so that everything goes back together in the correct position.

Next you have to remove the bolts holding the spring plate and the axle together, along with the bottom shock mounting bolt, and slacken the assembly off. Then remove the four bolts that hold the cover plate in place and take the plate off. You now have access to the torsion bar itself. Again, for reference purposes, mark the current position of the torsion bar and the trailing arm. Now, lift the spring plate with a jack off the bump stop and let it down slowly. This little operation needs to be done carefully because the spring plate is held under tension by the torsion spring.

The spring plate can then be removed from the splines on the outer ends of the torsion bar by hitting the latter gently with a hammer and when it's off, which may take some time and not a little bad language, the spring plate can be relocated one or two splines up from its more normal position. One spline will lower your Bus to a reasonable degree whereas two splines is plenty far enough. Notch it round four splines and your Bus will be seriously low. Then put everything back together in the reverse order in which it was removed.

Now fit a set of Bilstein, Koni or Spax shocks and the feel of your Bus on the road will be transformed. There is not very much wrong with the handling and roadholding of a Bus in stock form but a little modification here and there can dramatically improve it.

The next most logical stage is to change the stock VW steel wheels for a set of alloys. They won't make your Bus go detectably faster but they will certainly brighten up its appearance and, luckily, there's no shortage of choice. What constitutes a good-looking wheel is solely down to personal preference but, make no mistake, there is a vast difference in quality between wheels from different manufacturers. If you're buying a used set, be sure to check them thoroughly before you part with hard-earned cash. An alloy that has been 'kerbed' time and again is likely to contain hairline cracks even though they aren't visible to the human eye, and presents a potential danger for further use. Therefore, look carefully for small and large scrapes on the rims. Spin them around in your fingers to ensure that they run true. It's not an accurate method but a badly buckled wheel will be immediately apparent to you. Don't

Lowering the rear suspension is a relatively simple matter of rotating the torsion bars on their splines to the required height, in this case by a radical four notches.

Chromed steel wheels can look effective and are a good deal cheaper than alloys.

worry too much about surface corrosion because alloy cleans up really well with polishing or sandblasting, but reject any wheel that shows signs of deep corrosion. No matter how low the asking price, the safety risk is not worth it. With alloy wheels you get very much what you pay for, and if you have cash to spare it's worth paying for the best. Take a trip to BBS in Schiltach, Germany, and it will soon become clear why their products cost so much to buy. A set of alloys for your Bus needn't cost as much as BBS items though, far from it. Arguably the most popular choice (and the best looking) are EMPI-style 8- and 5-spoke wheels and the 5-spoke Fuchs items as fitted to Porsche 911s of the 1960s and '70s. Even secondhand the latter aren't cheap but they're of excellent quality and should last a lifetime if looked after properly.

Incidentally, if the wheels you want have four bolt holes rather than five, it will be necessary to buy a set of wheel adaptors which simply bolt on to the existing hubs. Most retail outlets specializing in

Low Samba with wide multi-spoke alloys, modified air–intake louvres and clean graphics.

EMPI-style 8- and 5-spoke wheels in 5½J width are stylish and suit Buses particularly well.

wheels normally stock adaptors too.

Stick to 5½J width and you won't foul the body-work. Go really wide and you will be into the realms of expensive low-profile tyres. Interestingly, really low-profile boots don't work especially well on Buses (or Bugs for that matter) particularly in wet weather when they make the roadholding 'skittish'. They simply put too much rubber on the road and in the long run they also impose excessive strain on the wheel bearings and other suspension components.

For the owner of a post-'79 Transporter, suspension lowering is a lot easier than for owners of traditional torsion-bar vehicles. All that's required is a shorter set of coil springs and, in the case of really radical lowering, a set of shorter-than-stock shocks. Shorter springs may not be available off the shelf but getting a set made up, or indeed modifying the existing springs to fit, is not beyond the scope of a good machine shop. Radical lowering will require the steering geometry to be re-set but that is a job for a VW specialist. Do not try it at home.

CAL LOOK & CUSTOMS

That the Volkswagen Transporter now plays a such a major role in youth culture is not entirely down to coincidence. It is after all the most practical, best-looking and most durable Bus around. It is also one of the safest and cheapest to buy and run. Spare parts are in plentiful supply even for early Splitties, and in the absence of genuine Volkswagen components there are quite literally tons of good quality reproduction parts available through an army of specialist suppliers.

But surely the same applies equally to the majority of Buses made by other manufacturers? Toyota, Nissan, Mercedes-Benz and many others also make excellent people and goods carriers. Ford, Renault and Citroën have all, in their time, launched first-class commercial vehicles and leisure-orientated Buses, and yet it is Volkswagen's immortal Type 2 that continues to capture the imagination of both those who are young and those still young at heart.

Every year Volkswagen Bus fanatics spend small

The chromed VW emblem and body mouldings are retained, but the American-spec bumpers, Porsche alloys and contrasting paint scheme all conspire to make one classy Bus.

Classic French-built Cal-look Panel-van is devoid of superfluous trim, has high quality pastel paintwork and a neat Rossi headlamp conversion. Note that the window frames have also been removed.

Lowered suspension and a colour-matched front bumper give this otherwise stock Splittie a more sporting appearance.

fortunes restoring, rebuilding, personalizing and customizing their vehicles – and why? Because Volkswagen has Style (spelt with a large capital 'S') and a charm of its own. No other vehicle of today or yesteryear exudes the same charisma, is penned with such simple beauty or lends itself so easily and naturally to the art of the customizer – except the Bug, of course.

A symbol of freedom and very much part of a uniform by which youth culture can be identified, VW Buses have been subjected since the 1960s to every kind of customizing imaginable. By far the most popular trend in the past 20 years has been towards creating and developing the Cal-look theme. Fashions in the automotive industry certainly come and go, but the Cal-look is the most enduring of all recent trends and deservedly so because in 'cleaning up' the original design it is seen by many as the ultimate expression of the VW way of life.

Cal-look is about making Volkswagens beautiful whilst at the same time retaining their practical virtues. Cal-look is about creating a 'head-turner' in an age of uniformity, dullness and conformity in car design. Borne out of the human desire to be different and individual, the Cal-look is fresh and bright. Like a David Hockney painting, all the character of the original subject is retained and well draughted, but the final execution, the top gloss is something special and personal. Cal-look is subtle and far from outrageous, but there are no written rules as to how a Cal-looker should be. That would rather defeat the object, but there are hallmarks, that single out and identify Cal-look style. They include a perfectly smooth paint job, preferably, but not always, in a pastel colour, a reworked interior, lowered suspension, a neat set of alloy wheels, maybe a smoothed-off dashboard, trick rear lights, one-piece windows and a sound system with sufficient power to do justice to the musical talents of Pearl Jam, Red Hot Chilli Peppers, ZZ Top and the Beach Boys.

Create your own Cal-looker to your own specification and design and you will soon have yet another unique version of the Volkswagen Bus.

Because Splitties are held in such high regard nowadays, few actually come in for the full treatment, the majority of owners being content to stick with lowering the suspension and restoring their precious Buses back to original condition. So why

This beautiful Microbus has been lowered and sits on some meaty rubber. The stunning palm tree mural typifies West Coast surf style.

Stock Pick-up sports simple but imaginative rainbow and floral graphics but retains German company name and business details for authenticity.

Fully kitted Camper has everything for the weekend including roof rack and rear bike rack, but is sufficiently lowered to give a hint of personalization.

Concours winning resto-Cal Splittie looks stock apart from the lowered suspension and alloy wheels.

Lowering the front end only (below) and retaining the standard ride height at the rear apes the drag racing trend.

A pink Cal-looker: perfect for posing.

Subtle colours and a carefully penned graphic design give Marc Maskery's 1962 Bus a touch of exotica.

Fadeaway V-over-W emblem is available from Volkswagen main dealers.

Three types of VW roundel; early flat type highlighted in lilac, stock white plastic and chrome. You can take your pick when it comes to personalization.

While restoring his Bus, Steve Newey confined the exterior personalization to a modern lilac and white paint scheme.

not choose a Bay or Wedge? They're just as much fun, they're cheaper to buy, and because there are so many still about no-one seems to mind a little artistic licence when it comes to personal customizing.

For the paintwork, it is dead easy to start with a clean sheet of paper and map out your own colour scheme. If you want to add graphics, incorporate them into your drawings. If they don't look right, start again until you come up with an idea that works. Keep everything as simple or as complex as you like, but history shows that straight lines usually work better on Buses than wild curves when it comes to adding graphic art.

These rear lights are flush with the sheet metal, a trick that involves little more than a day's work with a welding torch and some body filler.

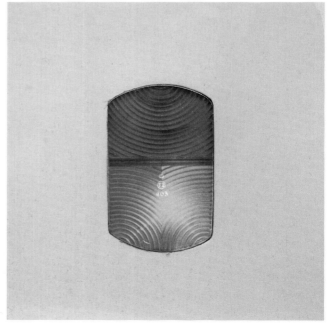

The well-proportioned lines of the Double-cab (above) make it ideal for customizing, but to restore one to this condition will cost plenty.

Lowered suspension, modern alloys, a tailor-made body kit and a mega sound system: this must be the ultimate customized Wedge (below).

Andy Rice's Cal-look Bay-window is ultra-low, smooth, a
concours winner, and has an open sunroof at the front.

This stock Bay-window Camper's paint scheme – yellow with pink details – is effective without body graphics.

Built for comfort, body-hugging bucket seats are easy to fit and need not cost a packet.

Top-of-the-range Corbeau GTS leather recliner is the ultimate in luxury.

The interior design can offer greater scope for the imagination to run riot. There are plenty of ready-made seats (Corbeau and Recaro do a great range) and interior panels available, but if none of them appeal to you why not make your own seat covers and panels up at home? Nothing could be easier. Even the original Volkswagen seats can look fantastic if you choose a good material to cover them. Leather has the advantage of being comfortable and easy to clean, and the smell off a leather-clad interior is heavenly, but don't under estimate the cost. Stick to doing the front cab seats if you're on a budget. Alternatively, seek out a scrapyard and buy a pair of seats from a modern car. Most cars, especially in the upper price range, are equipped with superb seats, and adapting them to fit a Bus is far from difficult.

Many a fabric store has provided inspiration for new headliners and interior designs, and a few square yards of dressmaking material could quickly turn your Bus into something quite exotic. The opportunities are endless, as evidenced by the show vehicles that walk away with the best prizes at concours.

This three-spoked alloy steering wheel is trimmed in vinyl and looks neat with the V-over-W emblem positioned off-centre on the horn button.

Of all the items you buy and fit to your Cal-looker, the steering wheel is probably going to be the most difficult and personal choice. After all, it is the one fitment that puts you in touch with the vehicle at all times when you're out cruising. A small diameter wheel is not totally out of the question because steering a Bus, even at parking speeds, is not exactly dif-

A smooth dashboard, bright interior panels and subtle colour-matching are hallmarks of the Cal-look.

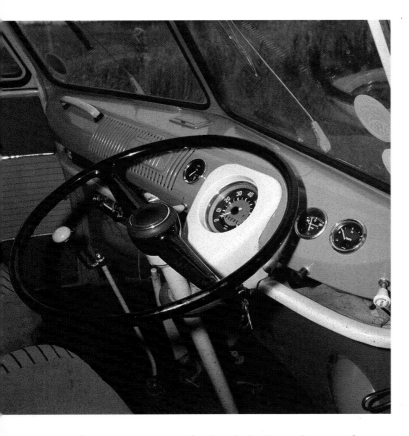

This Splittie dash panel (left) has a speckle finish and is enhanced with additional instruments. The gear shifter has a useful extension.

The extravagant use of colour (below) is a departure from true Cal-look, but there's no mistaking its individuality.

The dashboard is stock (above) but the face of the speedometer is highlighted in red, a typically Cal-look detail.

The traditional wooden fixtures are retained in this 1965 Camper, but the fabric for the seats and interior panels was chosen to create an English 'cottage' look.

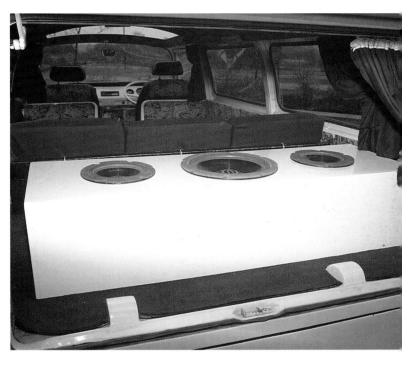

The interior of this Bay-window (below) has been transformed with inexpensive curtain fabrics.

Placing the hi-fi speakers in a purpose-built cabinet over the engine is a practical solution to a perennial problem.

ficult. Alloy spokes look great and a leather-trimmed rim will add a touch of class. Leather is also comfortable to handle, but if you object on ecological grounds vinyl does the job just as well.

If you can't stand looking at the stock dash, remove it and start again. A really good job involves welding in a new panel of sheet metal that incorporates a few well positioned apertures in which to install the speedometer and other gauges. The object is to achieve as smooth a look and finish as possible. No, a big tachometer is not really much use on a Bus unless you have a high-revving, fire-breathing engine, but the presence of one neatly fitted into the dash will certainly improve the overall appearance. An oil temperature gauge is probably the most useful instrument you can fit for rather obvious reasons.

Modified or stock, the engine bay should be spotlessly clean.

Have you ever wondered what your engine is doing back there when you're blasting down a motorway at full speed? Well, amongst other things, it's getting pretty damned hot. Unfortunately, fitting an oil gauge won't make it run any cooler but at least you can keep an eye on the temperature if, for some reason, your right foot just won't disconnect itself from the gas pedal. The most popular gauges are those made by VDO but the Smith's items fitted to several British saloon cars of the 1950s and '60s are, on the whole, more stylish. Paint the dash in the same colour as the external bodywork and the overall effect will look neat indeed. If you've applied graphics externally, why not do a repeat job in miniature

on the dash? Such tricks are classic Cal-look touches and on the whole they can't be improved upon, unless you know different.

The absence of chrome body trim has for many years been one of the distinguishing features of the Cal-look. It just has to come off, but store it away carefully, you may want to put it back on your vehicle one day. Some people actually get fed up with the appearance of their Buses without it. And the same applies to other stock items which are easy to dismiss in the excitement of converting a factory vehicle into a neat Looker. One neat trick is to reposition the rear light clusters so that they are flush with the bodywork. To do this, the lights must be removed. Cut out the sheet metal to which they are attached so that you are left with two round holes in the bodywork and weld in a metal plate behind the two holes on each side. Then smooth out the whole area with body filler and refit the light clusters.

Alternatively the lights can be recessed into the bodywork by the 'frenching' method. Again, you will need to remove the light clusters and a small amount of sheet metal and weld in short cylindrical tubes to the inside of the bodywork where the stock lenses normally sit. Having painted the tubes to match the body colour, the lights can then be screwed into position inside them. If you choose to fit non-Volkswagen lights, hang on to the originals in case you tire of the frenched items. The latter certainly look neat, but by their nature, the pods tend to retain rain water and may eventually rot away.

As mentioned elsewhere, when it comes to selecting a set of wheels and tyres the choice is almost unlimited. Classic Cal-look Buses wear EMPI style 5- or 8-spoke alloys but a set of Fuchs 5-spokes as fitted to early Porsche 911s are probably the first choice with the majority of folks if their cash can stretch that far. The Empi-style 'spokers' come in a variety of colours including white, black, gold and silver. Black and silver will match almost any bodywork colour but a little care is needed to achieve the right effect with white and gold.

From an aesthetic point of view, tyre choice is almost critical, and there isn't much point in spending a lot of time and money getting the paintwork and wheels right if you finish off with a set of skinny, high-profile cross-plies with a dubious country of origin. Go for a good set of radials with a reasonably low profile – but not too low if handling and roadholding are on your list of priorities.

So you've finished making the Looker of your dreams. It's sparkling in the early morning sunshine and ready for cruising. Enjoy it, keep it clean, maintain its mechanicals properly and it will serve you well for many years. The very essence of Cal-look is the expression of a simple, uncomplicated and happy lifestyle with no worries. Why not keep it that way?

CAMPER CONVERSIONS

A Volkswagen publicity shot from the early 1960s depicts a family enjoying a beach holiday with their Westfalia-converted 'Campmobile'. The roof-mounted luggage rack is now a rare accessory.

In the 1920s and '30s motoring folk who wanted to carry everything with them on long trips including the kitchen sink, but who weren't terribly keen on sleeping under canvas, bought a caravan and towed it behind the family car. Lightweight and small as most caravans of that era undoubtedly were, they often imposed insufferable burdens on underpowered tow-cars. An average 1930s British-built tin-top saloon could, in most instances, hardly pull its own weight up the steepest hills let alone drag a caravan at the same time, and to be fair, neither could a typical daily driver made in Germany, France or Italy.

Thanks to Volkswagen, the days of towing caravans and praying for a miracle half way up each hill were over - or at least they were for those who saw a Bus converted into a caravan as the answer to all their motoring problems. Directly after the Second World War, leisure time for the majority of people in Western Europe was pretty rare, but five or so years later, after the social and economic pressures began to ease up a little, more and more people became accustomed to taking time off work.

Weekends were precious, and for those who had saved up enough money to buy and run some form of motorized transport there was an increasingly wider choice. In 1951 the German coachbuilder, Westfalia, was the first to take a Volkswagen Kombi and turn it into a 'mobile home'. Westfalia's legendary 'Campingbox' started a whole new industry which today is worth millions in any currency you might care to mention and has been copied many thousands of times the world over. Established by Johann Bernhard Knobel in 1844 for the purpose of making agricultural implements, Westfalia swiftly moved on to making horse-drawn coaches by 1850, and founded its own paint and upholstery shop in 1887 in order to become fully independent of outside suppliers.

A highly successful company which expanded slowly, it began producing box trailers at the end of the 1930s and just six years later had moved into the world of caravan manufacture. Renowned for its high quality of workmanship, Westfalia was employing some 250 craftsmen by the time war broke out in 1939. At the end of hostilities, one of the firm's factories at Sandberg had been almost completely destroyed in Allied bombing raids, but work was quickly resumed and its first steel-plate caravan was exhibited at the 1947 Hanover Fair. In 1951 the first Campmobile was created, using a Volkswagen

The majority of Campers sold in North America were converted in Germany by Westfalia. Note the turret-like elevating roof.

A Westfalia conversion on an early 1960s Microbus included the side awning.

Transporter as its base, and by the end of that decade, in 1959, the 1,000th vehicle had left Westfalia's immaculate workshops. By the time it celebrated its 125th anniversary in 1969, Westfalia had produced 100,000 car trailers and 50,000 Campmobiles, extending its production of the latter to 100,000 by 1971.

The oil crisis saw the production of Campmobiles for export drop from 100 to 60 units per day, but by 1975 the company had recovered and exhibited the first Campmobile based on the Volkswagen LT Transporter. In its jubilee year, 1984, the company's 250,000th Campmobile was completed in September, and the following year Westfalia began its co-operation with the Ford Motor Company. These impressive figures – from one company alone – tell a lot about the popularity and appeal of the Volkswagen caravan.

A second home, an office in which to work, a mini-conference centre, a sportsman's changing room, a restaurant, a refuge in times of crisis: it is all of these things and a great deal more besides. A bewildering number of specialist companies have come up with their own ideas as to how the interior fittings and fixtures should be arranged, and more often than not they have been further improved or re-arranged by individual owners, which is why you will rarely find two identical Campers. Incidentally, one of the principal reasons why there are so few early Panelvans left these days is because so many were converted to caravans, again to individual designs.

The vast majority of designs, officially sanctioned by the factory or not, follow similar design tenets for the interior layout, and there are three basic types. There are those that cater solely for two people, those that are primarily intended for two adults and two children, and lastly there are conversions aimed at customers who want a vehicle that can be used for camping and load carrying at the same time.

As a general but by no means rigid rule, a double bed was installed above the engine area with a bench seat in front of the deck forming part of the bed. The cab seats and the bench provided seating for around five adults, with room for one other in an additional seat, facing either forwards or backwards, next to the side door. Refrigerators were rarely fitted in the early days and the cooker was likely to be a simple twin-burner gas-fired unit.

As time went on, the various conversions became

A unique Bug-on-Bus conversion. The Bug's roof retains opening quarter lights and windshield wipers.

more sophisticated and complex. Larger and more comprehensive fixtures were incorporated, but with such a limited area in which to install them, interior space was quickly used up and it was very much a case of the more you got, the less you had.

To increase headroom, elevating roofs were offered by a number of converters, the Westfalia unit being distinguished by sloping upwards towards the rear of the vehicle. Simple concertina-sided roofs and side-elevating roofs were popular with other converters, and some even have bunk beds built into them, but elevating roofs were always something of a bone of contention at the Volkswagen factory particularly in the late 1950s and '60s when every man and his dog seemed to be starting a company to offer camping conversions.

One of the reasons why so few companies were officially recognized by the factory is simply that by cutting a large hole in the roof of the vehicle for the purpose of fitting an elevating roof, a steel structural member had to be removed, which reduced the strength of the shell. Westfalia got around the problem by fitting a small roof that looked a little like a gun turret, while others took the view that Volkswagen were being overcautious about safety and went ahead with a more accommodating unit.

In the United States the vast majority of people bought Westfalias, but in Britain the most popular conversions, especially for Splitties, were the Devons produced by J.P. White of Sidmouth, which were offered in different levels of trim. The entry-level Devonette was equipped with two bench seats, a wardrobe unit, two cupboards in the rear and a cooker, and the Caravette included a water system, coolbox and additional cupboards. The range topping Torvette was similar to the Caravette save that it had a different cupboard arrangement, the cooker was more conveniently situated and there was a double cupboard in the rear.

Westfalia's elevating roof was sloped at an angle and offers limited headroom.

A hardworking Devon motor caravan earns its holidays in the sun

An early brochure from J.P. White of Sidmouth, England, whose Devon Campers were among the most successful British conversions.

The Martin Walter side-elevating roof is particularly easy to erect and gives masses of headroom.

Steve Saunders's restored Devon Caravette is still regularly used for cruising and camping.

A summer day and a perfect spot to bed down for the night. The Caravette was the mid-spec model in the Devon range.

Steve Saunders's Splittie has all the original Devon fittings including the optional side canopy. The modern fire extinguisher on the side door is essential equipment for all Campers.

By the mid 1960s, the Devon range had been considerably changed and improved. The standard Caravette based on the Microbus was equipped with a double bed for two adults and singles for two children, a twin-burner cooker with grille, a 7-gallon water tank, two tables, a food cooler, stainless steel cutlery for four people, a large awning in canvas, curtains for all the windows and natural oak woodwork for the cupboards and fittings. A Martin Walter side-elevating roof could be supplied at extra cost which not only offered further sleeping accommodation but gave excellent full standing headroom.

The only drawback of this very comprehensive conversion, as noted by *Practical Motorist* magazine in 1966, was interior condensation in cold damp weather. The author of the test, John Thorpe, wrote, 'Our van was equipped with a side-elevating roof in which were two more bunks folding out from the van sides. These proved to be unusable during the cold wet weather which we experienced, condensation on the plastic thoroughly wetting the bedding and freezing the occupants'. However, Mr Thorpe concluded, 'By the end of the week, we had all come to regard it as perfectly normal to climb in and out of the boxy-looking van when visiting friends and relations. I had found that it was as handy a runabout as any car, and much more so when it came to loading up the family shopping'. Incidentally, the Caravette in 1966 cost just £1,070.

Devon cab is stock apart from the gearshift extension and windshield spotlight, a once popular accessory for reading direction posts at night.

During the 1970s, there were dozens of different interior designs from the specialist converters. Here, the utility cabinet is positioned next to the sliding door, which restricts access to the rear seats, but standing room is generous.

The Canterbury Pitt was another popular conversion, similar to a Devon except that the Canterbury had a fold-up cooker mounted on the side door to allow for a full width rear seat. The Canterbury also had a little vanity unit in the rear for toiletries and a curtain over the wardrobe section in the rear. Canterbury Pitt prided itself on offering a second home on wheels and advertised its products as 'Private motoring in hotel comfort all the year round'. With up to eight seats and sleeping accommodation for up to seven, the Canterbury was a highly desirable Bus costing between £939 and £1,248 in 1966.

Produced by Martin Walter the Dormobile conversion had a kitchenette area across the top of the engine with the seats arranged conveniently in an 'L'

shape along the offside, and it was this same company that marketed a side-elevating roof containing two beds, a clever way of creating more sleeping accommodation. Not quite so clever, though, for the people sleeping below, because it has been known on exceptionally aged vehicles for the two upper beds to come crashing down without so much as 'good evening'. A sink unit, water tanks, cooker, cupboards, wardrobes and interior lighting came as standard and the elevating roof and additional beds

were offered as optional extras in 1963 when a Dormobile would have set you back just £820, or £925 for the four-berth model.

During the late 1950s, Danbury also offered conversions on Split-screen vehicles, but much of their work was involved with converting Panelvans, which means that they also put their own windows in. Danbury's approach to motor caravans in the 1960s was altogether different. They took the view that the Volkswagen Transporter was first and foremost a vehicle for the road and that the fixtures and fittings should not detract from this. On their 'Multicar' almost all the fittings were detachable so that the overall layout could be changed at will by the owner. The sink could be moved to make way for a

In this conversion, a much small cooker is fitted and access to the rear seats is much improved. There is an additional rear facing seat and the elevating roof is fitted with windows.

large seat. When not in use, the table legs could be unscrewed and the table top used as a platform for the main bed. Unusually, the Danbury also came with a teapot, frying pan, and a saucepan. *Autocar* magazine wrote of the Danbury, 'The Multicar looks more businesslike and less of a holiday vehicle'. The company, in its no nonsense approach, converted Panelvans for its regular models, but by the mid 1960s used Kombis as a base model more often than not.

The much larger Bay-window Campers appealed to a wider public, and by the end of the 1960s the concept of a well-fitted mobile home had become universally popular and a great variety of models was available.

Moortown Motors of Leeds offered two versions based on either the Kombi or the more luxuriously trimmed Microbus and both were exceptionally spacious. Both models had 6-gallon water tanks and a rocker-type pump with a pivoting spout that could be swung round to fill a door-mounted hand basin. The cooker and the hand basin could be used from outside or inside, a particularly useful feature when the optional extension tent was used. Fluorescent lighting came as standard equipment on the Microbus version but not on the Kombi. A most practical motor caravan, Moortown Splitties are now quite rare.

There were so many conversions around in the 1960s, differing one from the next in small details such as an extra cupboard here and a fire extinguisher there. By the middle of that decade, the cult of the motor caravan had grown enormously all over the world. In Britain, Europe, America, Africa and Australia, Volkswagens were converted for use as leisure vehicles in a bewildering number of different specifications. Many different types of wood and plastics were used for interior fittings by the specialist companies and van owners who didn't want to pay for the pleasure of someone else carrying out a 'high-tech' conversion for them, got on with the job of doing it themselves.

When the Bay-window model was introduced for the 1968 model year, the specialist companies had a field day because there was more room in which to exploit their design talents. Converters by and large continued to cater for two adults and two children or two adults on their own, and offered designs that allowed for the vehicle to double up as a people or goods carrier. Naturally, Westfalia continued as Volkswagen's official converter in Germany and their Campmobile for the 1968 model year was heralded by Volkswagen's loyal clientele and the press alike as the best Bus of its kind.

A six-passenger station wagon, the Campmobile was equipped with the customary high-quality fixtures and fittings. There were new storage lockers under the rear seat and alongside the sliding door, and the tilting elevating roof doubled as a child's bedroom. The kitchen sink was built into a recess on the top of the icebox and the cover for the pantry which was built into the side of the icebox cabinet folded upwards to provide a work surface. The centre of the vehicle was designed to provide seating for

Another Volkswagen publicity photograph showing that a well converted Camper really can be a home away from home. Unusually for the early 1970s, this model is equipped with a portable television. Note the rectangular concertina-sided elevating roof.

up to four people and there were curtains fitted to all the windows. A louvred side window was also fitted for the purpose of ventilating the interior while at the same time keeping rainwater out. A large tent which fitted to the side of the vehicle, was available as an optional extra.

In Britain, Martin Walter continued to produce the Dormobile, offering a side-elevating roof as a cost option at less than £100. When raised, the elevating roof gave around eight feet of headroom, the two upper bunks were stored at the sides of the roof and the two lower ones were formed by pulling a loop on the rear bench seat. An additional children's bunk could be specified as a cost option and fitted across the top of the inside of the cab. A neat and practical conversion, the Dormobile remained as popular as ever in Britain.

Devon continued offering brilliant conversions as always, and as time went on, their attention to making detail improvements became outstanding. Devons could even be specified with a full-length side-elevating roof. The interior fittings such as the cupboards were always well planned, and given the amount of equipment that came with each conversion it is quite remarkable that there was still plenty of space in the interior to move around without feeling cramped.

It made little difference in Europe, Britain or America that Volkswagen soldiered on in the early 1970s with comparatively underpowered engines in the Transporter range. By this time, there were plenty of different types of motor caravans from several motor manufacturers who fitted powerful engines and provided larger bodies with more cabin space and a greater variety of luxury fittings, yet the Volkswagen remained on top, often outselling competitors several times over. The Volkswagen was the right size. It was easy to park and easy to drive. Anything bigger proved a liability for people who were more used to driving cars than trucks. The air-cooled engine required less maintenance than a conventional engine and was rarely unreliable.

In South Africa, Jurgens Caravans marketed the Auto-Villa with a large overhanging body styled more along the lines of a traditional caravan and an extension on top of the cab roof. The caravan part of the body was made from aluminium supported on an aluminium framework and insulated with polystyrene foam; the interior was trimmed in Taiwan hardwood veneer. A dinette was installed in the rear with seating for up to six people which converted into sleeping berths. A double bunk was placed over the top of the cab and was reached by a stepladder.

By 1970, Volkswagen's Bus, in whatever form, was a much sought-after vehicle. Don Macdonald, writing in the *World Car Guide* in that same year, said, 'Well used VW Buses are threatening Detroit's traditional concept of the youth market. Again,

escape via a Bus is far less expensive and more promising in terms of birds and bees than being encumbered with a bucket-seated, thirsty-engined GTO or Scat-Pack Dodge. Admittedly, however, flower symbols and curtained windows seem to attract the police as readily as racing stripes'.

A particularly versatile American conversion was the Sportsmobile, from a company based in Andrews, Indiana, who offered to take your Bus and install all the bits and pieces at their factory, or alternatively provide customers with a kit of parts for home-installation. Including the space in the elevating roof, the Sportsmobile could sleep up to four adults and two children in comfort.

Without doubt, all of the Volkswagen camper conversions are good and can be used for a variety of different applications. There isn't such a thing as a badly converted Bus but some just happen to be a little more interesting than others. Amongst the rarest and most useful are the Kemperinks made in Holland. Kemperink produced their own versions of both Splitties and Bays and specialized in 'stretching' vehicles by up to four feet in length. Exactly how many long-wheelbase 'Kemps' were actually made is unclear, and the majority were converted for commercial rather than recreational use, but there are no more than ten examples known to exist in Britain. Just one or two have been fully kitted out with camping equipment, and because of their great length, must surely rank amongst the very best all-round Transporters.

The Oxford-based enthusiast and chairman of the British Type 2 Owners' Club, Simon Holloway, owns a 1975 Bay-window Kemperink which started life as a Pick-up truck. According to Simon, it was one of a pair specially commissioned to be built into a boxvan for a firm of bakers, and being right-hand drive, is rare even by Kemperink standards. Having spent most of its life performing duties on the south coast of England, the sea air had taken its toll on the bodywork by the time Simon acquired it in 1990, and almost a quarter of the bodywork needed replacing. Luckily, the roof panel is made of fibreglass. When the Dutch company converted it from a Pickup, they added a four-foot section to the middle of the bodywork and fitted a special cabin to the rear section, on a tubular steel frame. For good measure, four-foot doors were added to both the side and rear of the vehicle. As it was intended only for carrying bread, the 1600cc engine was deemed sufficiently powerful and is retained today. After being passed from the baker's firm to a grocer, the Kemperink acquired a couple of small windows in the sides of its bodywork and a eventually a home-made camping conversion.

Simon had his work cut out when it came to the Kemp's restoration, and he made a number of modifications to it as he went along, including the

After 12 years, production of the Bay-window Bus ended, but like the flared trousers worn by the happy couple in this period photograph, it would become fashionable again in the years to come.

An overhanging caravan body gives considerably more space than a conventional body. Note the air intake for the engine grafted in behind the rear side window.

Converted from a Pick-up by the specialist Dutch company, Kemperink, this Splittie is 4ft longer than stock and has a spacious aluminium body.

After its conversion from a Pick-up to a boxvan, Simon Holloway's 1975 Bay -window Kemperink was used as a bread delivery van, but because of its length and size it now serves as a spacious and versatile Camper.

removal of air ducting under the dashboard to make room for a water radiator as he intends one day to fit a diesel engine. 'Twelve years spent camping within the confines of a normal Bus taught me a lot about interior layout,' he says. 'What I wanted with the Kemperink was a safe place with space but also with as much useful equipment as possible.'

The specification list includes a three-way fridge, Tetford cassette toilet, a cooker with an oven, 240V mains electricity hook-up, twin batteries, hot water heater, kitchen sink plus drainer, a shower unit, twin gas bottle locker, a pressurized water system and sleeping accommodation for two adults, two kids and one exceptionally large Great Dane. 'The massive amount of extra space of the Kemperink makes this dream all possible. Imagine being able to get out of bed in the morning and putting your clothes on without hitting your head or stepping in something horrible.'

The Kemperink's interior equipment includes a fridge, toilet, mains electricity hook-up, twin gas bottle locker, pressurized water system and a shower unit. It sleeps up to four.

Access to the Kemperink's rear luggage bay is easy through the large 4ft tailgate.

By the time the third generation Transporters arrived, the motor caravan scene had changed almost completely. The Splittie, and Bay-window Buses had gathered a massive following and were popular with young and old alike but society had become more affluent and demanded more creature comforts and design sophistication. Volkswagen's new, bigger, wedge-shaped Bus was the answer, and once more the specialist companies engaged in conversion work had a field day. As everyone had come to expect from Volkswagen, the Wedge was beautifully finished, handled exceptionally well, was safe, smooth, fast, economical and provided an ideal alternative to more conventional forms of transport.

In Britain, the three official Volkswagen converters, Autohomes, Autosleepers and Richard Holdsworth produced Buses of unashamed luxury. Westfalia in Germany brought out their Vanagon, which *Car & Driver* magazine described as 'Probably

With revised bodywork, the third generation Campers are more spacious, better appointed and generally more luxurious than the Bay-window conversions.

Long distance driving is especially rewarding in a Wedge with its comfortable seats, modern dash layout and large, panoramic windshield.

the neatest, most compact conversion today. Elegant inside and out, there's genius in every drawer, every curtain snap, every hinge and every swivel.' On the Vanagon, the front seats could be swivelled through 180 degrees, which was useful at meal times, and the elevating roof tilted backwards instead of forwards as previously.

For 1980 Devon Conversions presented their Moonraker and Sundowner models, both comprehensively kitted out with every imaginable convenience including wardrobes, extension seats, dropdown work surfaces, all-over carpets, a twin-burner cooker, stainless steel sink unit and a refrigerator. The upholstery was as good as you would find in the average home, and aloft, in the elevating roof, there were two solid-based mattresses. A Porta-Potti chemical toilet was specified as an optional extra.

Danbury's Wedge conversion was especially interesting because it was the first motorized caravan to be fitted with a power-operated elevating roof. It was only necessary to push a button, and as the manufacturers stated in their sales literature, 'Even a child could operate it - which is why we have housed the switch in a lockable cupboard'. Danbury's approach to converting the Wedge to camping mode was as practical as ever. All the cupboard doors were crank-hinged to fold back flush against the units for greater safety, and the upholstery was in a hardwearing and easy-clean material. Fitted with masses of equipment, the Danbury was a first class dual-purpose vehicle and was competitively priced as usual.

When the air-cooled Buses reached the end of the road and were replaced by the water-cooled variety, secondhand values remained relatively high and continue to do so today. The water-cooled engines are quieter and more powerful, but for many Bus fans nothing will ever replace the magic of the traditional flat-four. If you are looking to buy a low-mileage example in good condition, you can still expect to pay plenty for it and even tatty, high-mileage specimens retain their value better than the majority of saloon cars of original comparable value.

Curiously, the world of motor caravans is one where, despite their considerable efforts, the Japanese manufacturers have never managed to topple Volkswagen as the world's number one choice. Splitties, Bays and Wedges alike all led the rest of the world in the motor caravan field, which is why today these wonderful vehicles have such a well-deserved following.

The British Devon Camper, with its plush velour seats, wall-to-wall carpets and high quality cabinets, typically caters for the demands of the modern age.

During the conversion of this Panelvan to a Camper, a fibreglass roof was bonded to the main body structure to increase headroom and sleeping accommodation.

TRANSPORTER HISTORY IN BRIEF

Major Hirst of the Royal Electrical and Mechanical Engineers took command of the Volkswagen factory at Wolfsburg in August 1945. Production of the Bug began. Internal transport at the factory was limited to a small number of electric vehicles. Hirst borrowed forklift trucks from the British army for a brief period and eventually replaced them with a crudely constructed flat-bed truck utilizing a Bug platform with a cab at the rear placed over the engine.

Ben Pon, the Dutch Volkswagen importer, saw one of these vehicles on a visit to the factory at Wolfsburg in 1948 and made a simple sketch, along with some notes, as to how a road-going Transporter might look.

His ideas were discussed with Heinz Nordhoff, who had been appointed managing director of the factory on January 1 1948.

Nordhoff ordered prototypes to be built and tested and in February 1950, the first Transporter rolls off the Wolfsburg assembly line. In March, mass-production of the Panelvan gets under way and in May, the Kombi follows with, or without seats. The Bus version was introduced in June as a 7-, 8- or 9-seater. An ambulance version was launched in November.

Original Specification

Dimensions 415cm/163in (l), 166cm/65in (w), 190cm/75in (h).
Wheelbase 240cm/94.5in
Engine capacity 1131cc
Bore × stroke 75 × 64mm
Compression ratio 5.8:1
Max power 25bhp at 3300rpm
Max torque 51lb/ft at 2000rpm
Empty weight 975kg/2150lb
Load capacity 750kg/165lb
Top speed 56mph
Acceleration 25-50mph loaded in 80 secs

1952 Pick-up launched. Necessitated relocation of spare wheel and fuel tank. Storage locker below platform. Synchromesh on top three gears.

1954 Engine enlarged to 1192cc, 30bhp. Compression ratio raised to 6.1:1. Right-hand drive available on all models.

1955 Major bodywork revisions to all models similar to those of the Pick-up in 1952. Spare wheel located behind driver's seat, fuel tank above gearbox with filler on outside of vehicle. This allowed lowering of engine deck and fitment of tailgate hatch above the engine lid. New full width dashboard, previously exclusive to de luxe version. New ventilation system with fresh air intakes above windshield giving peaked front to cab. 15in wheels replace 16in.

1956 Production transferred from Wolfsburg to Hanover. The new factory employed 5000 people and produced 250 vans per day.

1958 Double-cab (or Crew-cab) six-seat Pick-up launched.

1959 Engine redesigned. New crankcase allows for removal of generator pedestal, exhaust system improved. Synchromesh on all gears.

1960 Flashing indicators replace semaphores. Engine power increased to 34bhp. Compression ratio increased to 7.0:1. In the first 10 years of its production life, 678,000 Transporters were manufactured of which there were 243,000 Panelvans (35.8 per cent), 152,000 Kombis (22.4 per cent), 148,000 Buses (21.8 per cent), 129,000 Pick-ups (19 per cent) and 6000 special models (1 per cent).

1961 1,000,000th Transporter delivered in August.

1962 High-roof van introduced with six cubic metres load volume. Type 3 engine fitted for USA with a vertical fan housing. Heating improved, Eberspächer heater optional.

1963 1497cc 42bhp engine launched. New axles, new brakes, new 14in wheels, 1000kg/2205lb payload. Major bodywork revisions include wider rear hatch, new lights and indicators.

1967 New model introduced August. New body shape with one-piece curved windshield. Sliding side doors standard. High-roof van gets synthetic roof lining. Double-jointed rear axle. 1.6-litre 47bhp engine.

1968 High-roof van gets fibreglass roof.

1969 Doors strengthened, collapsible steering column introduced.

1970 Dual-port cylinder heads improve performance.

1971 New 1.7-litre 66bhp engine with cooling blower on nose of crankshaft to save space. Both 1.6- and 1.7-litre engines comply with US emission regulations.

1972 'Crunch zone' introduced with deformation parts in cab floor. Automatic 'box option except on Pick-up.

1973 Daily production reaches record 1200 vehicles. New 1.8-litre 68bhp engine introduced.

1975 1.8-litre engine enlarged to 2 litres 70bhp, permitted vehicle weight rises to 2500kg/5512lb.

1976 Partition walls in load area removed to allow greater adjustment of front seats.

1978 Special series 8-seater Bus made with metallic silver paintwork.

1979 Third generation Transporter announced.

1982 End of production of air-cooled Transporters in Germany.

Engine sizes and power output

1949
1131cc
bore 75mm
stroke 64mm
25bhp at 3300rpm

1954
1192cc
bore 77mm
stroke 64mm
30bhp at 3400rpm

1959
1192cc
bore 77mm
stroke 64mm
34bhp at 3700rpm

1963
1497cc
bore 83mm
stroke 69mm
42bhp at 3800rpm

1965
1497cc
bore 83mm
stroke 69mm
44bhp at 4000rpm

1967
1584cc
bore 85.5mm
stroke 69mm
47bhp at 4000rpm

1970
1584cc
bore 85.5mm
stroke 69mm
50bhp at 4000rpm

1971
1679cc
bore 90mm
stroke 66mm
66bhp at 4800rpm

1973
1795cc
bore 93mm
stroke 66mm
68bhp at 4200rpm

1975
1970cc
bore 94mm
stroke 71mm
70bhp at 4200rpm

Transporter body types

PANELVAN with seating in the cab only and without windows in the bodywork shrouding the load area. Designed specifically as a load carrier, many were converted into Campers by specialist companies and individuals.

KOMBI with side windows and removable seats in the load area. Upmarket Microbus version offered as a 7-, 8- or 9-seater with improved level of trim and 'Samba' with additional windows installed in the roof.

PICK-UP truck has separate cab, a flat-bed load area with collapsible sides and storage lockers for tools below bed. Spare wheel and fuel tank relocated in design to allow for low load height.

DOUBLE-CAB PICK-UP similar to conventional Pick-up but with extended cab and additional seating for up to six people and correspondingly shorter load area.

HIGH-ROOF Transporter based on Panelvan but with extended high roof. Aimed at clothing and other trades with specialist needs.

CAMPER kitted out with special equipment for leisure activities. Westfalia official converters in Germany sanctioned by Volkswagen but dozens of different types around the world.

AMBULANCE version built by Volkswagen in Germany for home market and appropriately kitted out.

SPECIAL versions built by Volkswagen for German public services including the post office, fire service and forestry commission. Majority based on Pick-up and Panelvan.